The **TOTAL** MARRIAGE

A guide to successful marriage

by Jeffrey and Pattiejean Brown

ABBREVIATIONS

KJV King James Version (1611).

LB Living Bible
TYNDALE HOUSE, 1971

NASB New American Standard Bible
THE LOCKMAN FOUNDATON, 1960

NIV New International Version
HODDER AND STOUGHTON, 1979

JBP J. B. Phillips, The New Testament in Modern English
COLLINS, 1972

RAV Revised Authorised Version
SAMUEL BAGSTER & SONS LTD., 1982

Scripture passages not indicated are the author's own paraphrase.

ISBN 1-873796-75-7

Copyright © 1999
Autumn House Publishing
All rights reserved.
No part of this publication
may be reproduced in any form
without prior permission
from the publisher.

Printed in England
for
AUTUMN HOUSE
Grantham, England

Second printing 1999

The TOTAL MARRIAGE

by JEFFREY and PATTIEJEAN BROWN

Jeffrey and Pattiejean Brown conduct Relationship Seminars for marital and premarital couples and singles. Pattie is a nursing assistant and secretary while Jeff teaches pastoral counselling, marriage and family life courses at undergraduate and postgraduate levels. He is an ordained minister and certified marriage counsellor with a PhD from Andrews University in Michigan. They have two children, Kristle and Jamel.

EDITOR
DAVID MARSHALL, BA PhD

MEDICAL EDITORS
Eileen Baildam, MD DCH MRCGP FRCP FRCPCH
Karen Shelbourn, MEd BA DipN(Lond) CertEd RGN

CONSULTING EDITORS
Karen Holford, MA, and Bernie Holford, MDiv,
Family Life Educators and Counsellors
Isobel Webster, MA, and Bryan Webster, MA, Family Counsellors
Britta and Hugh Dunton, MA PhD, Author and family consultant
Sheila and Mike Stickland, MA, Discovery Centre

This book is dedicated to
our mothers
Mrs Isabelle McMahon and Mrs Carmen Brown
our stepmother
Mrs Launa Brown
our fathers
Mr Charles McMahon and Dr Maurice Brown
and our grandparents
Ms Ivy Powell, Mrs Myrtle McMahon, the late
Mr Donald McMahon
and the late Mr & Mrs George and
Berneice Darrell

We would like to thank each one of you
for taking so much effort and making
so many sacrifices to give us a happy
and safe childhood.
We each have such fond memories of
family togetherness.
Our ability to enjoy marriage and pass on
Christian values to our children is because of
what you handed down to us.
We owe you a debt of gratitude we
can never repay.
Just know that your struggles, tears,
and prayers were worth it.

We love you.
Jeffrey and Pattiejean Brown

The TOTAL MARRIAGE

CONTENTS

WHAT'S LOVE GOT TO DO WITH IT?

2 | **PAGE 20**

3 | **PAGE 32**

1 | **PAGE 8**

THE BURDENS AND BLESSINGS OF SINGLENESS

MARRIAGE: IDEAL, ORDEAL OR NEW DEAL?

PAGE 50

IT TAKES TWO TO SUBMIT

 PAGE 69

TWENTY YEARS, NO ARGUMENT. REALLY?

 PAGE 86

MARITAL SEX, GOD'S WEDDING GIFT

7 **PAGE 100**

CHILDREN, THE GIFT OF MARRIAGE

8 **PAGE 127**

YOU CAN LOVE AGAIN

9 **PAGE 144**

'AS I HAVE LOVED YOU'

10 **PAGE 156**

LIVING LIFE TO THE FULL

 Marriage: ideal, ordeal or new deal?

'Men ought to give their wives the love they naturally have for their own bodies. The love a man gives his wife is the extending of his love for himself to enfold her. Nobody ever hates or neglects his own body; he feeds it and looks after it. And that is what Christ does for his body, the Church. And we are all members of that body, we are his flesh and blood! For this cause shall a man leave his father and mother, and shall cleave to his wife; and the twain shall become one flesh. The marriage relationship is doubtless a great mystery, but I am speaking of something deeper still – the marriage of Christ and his Church. In practice what I have said amounts to this: let every one of you who is a husband love his wife as he loves himself, and let the wife reverence her husband.'
EPHESIANS 5:28-33, JBP.

Cinderella and marriage

The story is told of a little girl listening to the wonderful story of Cinderella. The 6-year-old was captivated by the story of the little waif doing the hard kitchen work of a household.

As the story unfolds, Cinderella makes her way to a beautiful ball and dances till midnight. According to the fairy, she must scurry back before she loses all the beauty and splendour of her ballgown. As the old clock begins to strike twelve, she dashes down the stairs. In her hurry she leaves behind her a little slipper. At the stroke of twelve all anyone sees is a little waif – no longer beautiful and splendid – making her way through the streets, and a few mice scattered here and there.

The little girl listening to the story of Cinderella was just captivated. Her mother continued with the story: 'Do you know what happened to Cinderella in the end? She lived happily ever after.' The little girl said, *'Oh, no she didn't. She got married!'*

Somehow, in that child's mind, the ideas of 'getting married' and 'living happily ever after' didn't quite fit together! One person said, 'When I got married, I was looking for an ideal. Then it became an ordeal. Now I want a new deal!' The same David who fought the giant Goliath knew that there would also be giants to conquer within marriage. He looked at the problem and realized that we need more than human help if our marriage is not going to end up where millions of others have. So he wrote in Psalm 127:1: 'Unless the Lord builds the house, they labour in vain who build it.' (RAV.)

Couples think they are perfect for each other on the day they get married. After about four weeks of wedded bliss, Maxine had no idea why Steve insisted that she fold the bath towels as his mother always had. Then there was Errol, whose obsession with having the car washed every Friday just annoyed Yvonne. Why couldn't they just wash it when it was dirty? And finally, Joyce, who just loved getting up at five o'clock to go and watch Leroy fishing – that is, *before* they got married. *After*wards she thought it was the most foolish thing in the world. Now I believe in premarital counselling. Couples should understand the issues before they enter into a permanent relationship. But do not think, just because you talked a few things over before marriage, that you necessarily know each other. *After* the wedding comes the marriage. What you see is not always what you get.

Dreaming and waking up
You see, when you're courting you see each other at your best. The girl spends hours getting ready, fixing her hair and her face; then there are her nails and on and on. And what about the man? Love will make him do strange things. It has been said that love will make you shine your shoes, brush your hair, and comb your teeth! But

In the courtship stage the girl will sometimes spend hours in preparation. She wants to make the best possible impression.

When the wedding and 'honeymoon phase' are over both partners wake up – literally and metaphorically – to an unglamorous image of their spouse which represents mundane reality.

after a wedding comes the marriage. When the wedding night is over, you wake up. What happened to the Paco Rabane aftershave and Chanel Number 5 perfume? In their place you have morning breath and scratchy whiskers. (And, before you know it, maybe even false teeth and false hair!) You wake up! The rude awakening may sound funny, but it is real. Marriage will make you wake up.

One romantic songwriter wrote, 'All I do the whole day through is dream of you; When night comes on I still go on dreaming of you.' Well, you're married now and it's morning time, so wake up, dreamer! There's a leak in the water pipe! Dinner's got to be prepared and she's out working! She's just heard another noise downstairs! Wake up, dreamer! 'Unless the Lord builds the house, they labour in vain who build it.' There's a type of love that lasts a lifetime. And there's another type of love that can scarcely survive the honeymoon. There's the popular or worldly kind of love, based on *contentment*, and there's the less popular Christian love, which is based on *commitment*.

Contentment or commitment?

You've seen them on TV: somebody's advertising a new broom or mop. And they'll dress up the girl so that she looks as if she has just stepped from the pages of *Good Housekeeping* or *Ebony*. She'll have her little mop and she'll be moving it back and forth with a perfect smile. That's not the way floors are washed in most houses. We do it with curlers in our hair, on our hands and knees. You see, with marriage, it may not always be pleasant, it won't always be easy, it may be a struggle, but it will always be worth it.

Worldly love emphasizes contentment; Christian love emphasizes commitment: choosing to love in spite of how your spouse talks, acts, or feels. Consider the following dialogue:

Husband: 'Darling, don't be upset. You know I've never found anyone who meets all my needs better than you do.'

Wife *(tearfully)*: 'But what if you did?'

Contentment or commitment? There are husbands who have found other women who they say have 'understood' them better than have their wives. Some, in middle age, have left behind home and children for that so-called greater understanding. There are wives who have met other men. They say these men have made them feel more 'important' and 'significant' than have their patronizing husbands. They've left behind housework and mums-and-toddlers' groups for roles that seemed more adventurous. What's the answer?

The psalmist David's words come back to us: 'Unless the Lord build the house, they labour in vain who build it.' I used to think this text meant: As long as we are both Christians it will be all right. I've had to change my opinion. One person wrote a song based on these words: 'Unless the Lord builds the house, they labour in vain to try and stop the rain from falling in.' I now believe the text means: As long as contentment is uppermost in your mind, the rain will fall in; and as long as commitment is low on your agenda, the rain will fall in.

Rights or responsibilities?
Society spreads around the rumour that life owes you something. That somehow you deserve the best out of life. Can't afford a holiday in the sun? Go anyway. Charge it; you owe it to yourself! Can't get that washing machine you've been wanting, like Mrs Smith's? The 'Buy Now Pay Later' scheme will rescue you. You *deserve* it. Things not working out at home? Why stay?

Contentment or *commitment?*

The truth is, life actually owes us nothing, we owe God everything. We live in an age of rights and demands, but marriage is not about rights. You can search through all the pages of Scripture and you'll find nothing about your rights. The Bible doesn't talk about rights, it talks about responsibilities. We have no right to life; that's given to us as a gift from our Creator. We have no right to happiness; that's a by-product of love and service. We have no right

The advertising industry creates the impression that there are things couples have a right to expect; everything from holidays in the sun to dishwashers. Reality, by contrast, requires us to live within tight budgets.

to forgiveness and love; in fact, we deserve just the opposite.

You see, in the final analysis, marriage has nothing to do with Cinderella. It is not our promise to each other that keeps the marriage together; it is God's promise that He will never leave us nor forsake us. Scripture records that God kept His promise in the person of Jesus Christ, who provided a model of love and fidelity unique and unparalleled: 'Having loved his own who were in the world, he now showed them the full extent of his love, he loved them to the end' (John 13:1, see NIV, RAV); 'I have given you an example, that you should do as I have done' (John 13:15, RAV). Christ now commands us to make and keep our promises. A marriage is created by the promises of two people who care enough to share. Your home will be kept together, not because being married is so much fun, but because two people dared enough to make – and dared enough to keep – their promises.

CULTURAL VARIATIONS

It is recognized today that family studies cannot be confined simply to the Western family because Western family patterns are minority patterns. The vast majority of families live under other cultures and have different backgrounds. Aceves and King, in their book *Cultural Anthropology*, acknowledge further: 'Few societies view marriage as Americans often view it – as a private matter between two people. Marriage creates important bonds between individuals and also between kin groups, in most societies.' Thus the often-used term 'minority' has now been called into question, the preference being to show Blacks, Asians and Hispanics as part of the world's *majority* cultures from which all cultures can receive great benefit.

MARRIAGE FACTORS HELD IN COMMON BY ALL CULTURES

Some approximation to monogamy (one husband, one wife)

A relatively strong tie between mother and child, at least during the child's early years

No unregulated promiscuity (though the Western World is considered by others to be indiscriminate and uncontrolled)

Functions of marriage: procreation, orientation, division of labour between the sexes, status-giving

The extended family

It comes as a surprise to some to hear that the extended family was a feature of most cultures until the Industrial Revolution. It was the onset of industrialization that began to reduce the extended family to the nuclear family. With increased mobility came a new emphasis on independence in family living. A shift occurred from mutual person-to-person concern and service to greater individualism and the development of a strong profit motive. The Western family model, with its personalized focus, led to a more individualistic society than the community-oriented nature of the African family. Western family patterns became conjugal and nuclear; African family patterns remained consanguine and extended.

African and Western

In many ways Western family life follows that of the ancient Greeks, and African family life follows that of the ancient Hebrews. Industrialization, Westernization, education, urbanization, and even Westernized Christianity have moved the contemporary African family away from the biblical model, rather than towards it. South African church leader Dr V. S. Wakaba maintains: 'The African family should not be

The biblical family was nearer to the African than the Western model; the extended family in which grandparents, parents, uncles and aunts, cousins and siblings are very much part of the picture.

contrasted with the Western family, in which the latter is held to rotate to the nuclear family. In ancient Israel, marriage would have been classified as "African" rather than "Western".' John Mbiti, in his book *Love and Marriage in Africa*, stretches the perimeters of marriage by stating that, 'Marriage is not just an affair of two individuals alone. You do not just marry one man or one woman.' African family life includes not only spouse but relatives, friends, work associates and club or church members.

While culture is very significant, let us consider the Bible's teaching on marriage.

THE BIBLICAL CONCEPT OF MARRIAGE

One (female) author says, 'The husband is the manager, and the wife is the assistant manager. She is comfortable in sharing her suggestions concerning the management of the company and is not upset when she is overruled.' I don't know that we would all agree with this, but Christians have generally embraced a traditional, hierarchical pattern of marriage. There are three phases in biblical history or acts of the biblical drama: creation, fall, and redemption.

❏ **Creation.** In Genesis 2:18 we find the word 'helper'. The biblical understanding of a 'helper' is not an assistant, a supporter, someone occupying merely a secondary position. The Hebrew word for 'helper' is used overwhelmingly in the Old Testament to describe God Himself. Hence it is a term that cannot be used to signify subordinate female roles.

God, the Helper (see Exodus 18:4) provided a helper to deliver the man from aloneness. Indeed, Adam and Eve enjoyed, before the Fall, a relationship of full mutuality in equality.

❏ **Fall.** Genesis 3 is the biblical record of the fall of humankind. Their sin resulted in dire consequences for their relationship: the husband would now rule over the wife. The fact that this is a new development lets us know that it was *not* what God had originally determined for the relationship but, so that harmony could continue to exist, the man was chosen as the leader. Ruling, then, is introduced as a consequence of the Fall. Man was not to have unholy dominion over his wife, but God foresaw that this would be the result. God is describing the results of sin, rather than saying what ought to be. Genesis 3:16 becomes God's description, not His prescription.

The 'he shall rule over you' should not be thought of as prescribing God's will any more than death may be regarded as God's will for humankind. The statement is not a licence for male supremacy, it is actually a condemnation of that very pattern. Subjugation and supremacy are perversions of creation.

So in God's garden, permeated

by trust, there is *mutuality* and *equality*. In God's garden now, infiltrated by distrust, there is *control* and *distortion*, a distortion which can in no way be accepted as the will of the Gardener.

At no point was it ever God's intention that the husband should dominate a totally submissive wife.

❏ **Redemption.** The redemption period began when Jesus came to earth. He came to restore everything that the Fall put in jeopardy, including a balanced and harmonious marriage. There are two statements of Scripture which are the foundation for what Christian marriage ought and ought not to be:

'it shall not be so among you' (Matthew 20:26, RAV);
'as I have loved you' (John 13:34, RAV).

What Jesus is saying is that there is to be a radically different emphasis in Christian relationships compared with those of the world. When your marriage partner promises to stay with you for life, the fact that he's a Christian ought to mean that, God helping him, he's going to do just that.

> ### A COVENANT
> may be defined as a promise or commitment binding two parties to one another unconditionally

Contract or covenant?

We hear a lot about marriage contracts today. The world is caught up in premarriage agreements and prenuptial contracts. A senior tax partner in New York said, 'Today at least 60 per cent of my clients have a prenuptial agreement.'

Prenuptial agreements are contracts that specify who gets what if a marriage falls apart. One friend of a soon-to-be-married popular female singer said, 'She loves him, yes, but ain't nobody going to get all her money.' Worldly love is built on a contract, Christian love is built on a covenant. A divorce lawyer in New York states that, 'Trust is involved in making a marriage work, and a prenuptial says, I don't trust you.'

Because Jesus has united or promised Himself to us, we can promise or covenant ourselves to one another. While the nature of a contract is something for something, the nature of a covenant is unconditional commitment. Covenant marriage exposes a radical difference in contemporary foundations of love. Covenant marriage happens when two people have made a commitment to Jesus Christ and to each other. Covenant marriage aims to restore God's original purpose for the family, no longer exclusive and inward-looking, but inclusive, using the richness of the marriage relationship to benefit others.

'You give 50 per cent and I'll give 50 per cent.' Sounds fair, doesn't it? But the emphasis in Christian relationships goes way beyond equality, all the way to oneness. That's what Jesus wants above all for us – oneness (see John 17:21 and 1 Corinthians 12:12). The bone taken from the side of Adam to make Eve signified a oneness far deeper than equality. I'm not looking over my shoulder to check if you are giving your 50 per cent, then I'll give mine; I'm giving 100 per cent, because that's what Jesus gave for me. Dr Ken Mulzac points out in his book, *Praying with Power*, that when the Bible talks about love it is spontaneous love which is shared whether or not the person is worth loving, simply because, since I've been born again, it's my (new) nature just to love!

So marriage is not an if-then alliance. Christian marriage is an in-spite-of, anyhow, regardless, nevertheless relationship. Yes, you're right. We do seem to do things differently. Sometimes we don't seem to be compatible. We *are* going through a rough patch, NEVERTHELESS . . . we're going to see it through. That's *Christian* marriage!

Covenant marriage will not necessarily be accepted or understood by today's popular culture; but then Christianity does not expect always to be understood. One of its leaders once said, 'The message of the cross is foolishness to those who are perishing, but to us who are being saved it is the power of God.' (1 Corinthians 1:18, RAV.)

> *'The Christian faith often operates with a lack of evidence that seems ridiculous to the rest of the world. It often seems to contradict the plain facts with a foolhardy 'nevertheless'. Such foolhardiness is built into our faith, because we proceed on the irrational assumption that God the Son has become a man among us, and we stake our lives on nothing but the story of the crucifixion and resurrection of that Son. . . . We entertain the seemingly ridiculous notions that nothing can separate us from the love of God, that He is working out a good purpose for us even when we are suffering or in pain. . . . Foolish? Yes, indeed it is foolish, but nevertheless true.'*
>
> ELIZABETH ACHTEMEIER, *THE COMMITTED MARRIAGE.*

LOVEWORK ON CHAPTER 1
COMPARING OUR STRENGTHS

1. Look at the list below and tick the strengths you see in each other.
2. Spend time complimenting each other on these strengths (refuse to hear comments from your spouse on number 3 if you have not been pampered in number 2!).
3. Are there any of these strengths that irritate you from time to time?

SANGUINE (POPULAR)	CHOLERIC (POWERFUL)	MELANCHOLY (PASSIONATE)	PHLEGMATIC (PEACEFUL)
Life of the party	Born leader	Talented and creative	Easygoing
Storyteller	Dynamic	Deep thinker	Cool, calm and collected
Very enthusiastic	Quick thinking	Faithful and devoted	Diplomatic
Good sense of humour	Competitive	Excellent listener	Dry humour
Very friendly	Confident	Sensitive to others	Unruffled
Lives for the present	Strong-willed	Detail-oriented	Very practical

Look at the pictures below.
Which picture best describes you/your partner? Have fun!

2 What's love got to do with it?

'Live your lives in love – the same sort of love which Christ gives us and which he perfectly expressed when he gave himself up for us in sacrifice to God. But as for sexual immorality in all its forms, and the itch to get your hands on what belongs to other people – don't even talk about such things; they are no fit subjects for Christians to talk about.'

EPHESIANS 5:2-4, JBP.

Holy Word or Hollywood?

How would you describe love? One person said, 'Love is like coals of fire; together they glow and burn; separated they die.' A second person said, 'Love is a feeling you feel when you feel you're going to get a feeling you never felt before.' A man who loved long words said, 'Love is a heterogenous conglomeration of absurdity calculated to bamboozle the anatomy of the individual who becomes intoxicated with its abominable and irresistible power.' And a fourth person said: 'Love is the only thing I know that will make a young boy act like an old man, and an old man act like a young boy. Love is the only thing I know that will make a young woman's heart go weak and an old woman's heart grow strong. Love is the only thing I know that will make a foolish man act wise and a wise man act like a fool, love!'

But what *is* love? Don't let Hollywood's definition of love distort your realities.

Bone of my bone

When God made the world and all the vegetation and living creatures, after each creation day He declared, 'It is good.' But *then* God made man and woman – man *and* woman – and He declared that it wasn't just good, it was *very* good. When Adam saw Eve he declared, 'This is, in fact, bone of my bone, flesh of my flesh.' Adam was shouting for joy! He was in love! But what *is* love?

A little boy was telling his parents about the creation of Adam and Eve. He had been learning about it in church. 'The teacher told us about how God made the first man – and the first woman. He made the man first – and the man got lonely for somebody to talk to. So God rocked him to sleep. And then He took out the man's brains and made a woman of them.' No, that's not what happened! He took a bone from Adam's side.

God didn't take the bone from Adam's head! That would have meant that the woman could henpeck her husband. God didn't take the bone from the foot either. That would have sent a message to men that it's all right to trample on their wives; to use, misuse, and abuse them. Today there's so much spouse abuse going on. Notice I said *spouse* abuse. Not just wife abuse. In Birmingham, in Britain's West Midlands, they have opened the first home for battered husbands, so you'd better treat each other right! However, I do not dispute that wife abuse is by far the more prevalent form of spouse abuse.

Notice, God took one rib and not two. Had He taken two ribs some men might have thought they could have a wife – *and* a girlfriend! No, God took *one* rib. He took the bone from the side, which means that the wife is equal to the husband. From under his arm, which means he's supposed to protect her. From near his heart, which means he's supposed to love her. So what *is* love?

Falling in love
Many people wonder if there is

God's ideal is marriage as a relationship in which two people are committed – *exclusively* committed – to one another. There is no room for third parties.

only one Mr Right or Mrs Right out there whom God has individually designed just for them. Psychologists tell us, however, that if you are a well-adjusted person you could be happily married to a number of individuals. Not at the same time, though! Pause for

> 'It is commonly said that a man and a woman fall in love and get married. In fact we climb up the ladder of love and mutual understanding. We climb inch by inch, day by day, year after year – climbing into the fullness of self-sacrificing love so clearly expressed on Calvary, but only gradually understood by us as we share it with each other.'
>
> *ANONYMOUS*

thought: 'It is the great mystery of human love which makes two hearts beat as one.' It's a mystery; and some don't see how it can be done. They don't see how two people can be committed – *exclusively* committed – for the rest of their lives. That's why I don't believe in falling in love.

It's easy to fall in love with someone on the TV screen. In a magazine. Someone in another church. Another town. Someone you don't see very often. Someone whose faults you don't really know. Someone whose weaknesses you don't really see. Someone who looks perfect every time you see them. It's easy to fall in love with such a person. But with real love you don't fall, *you climb!*

Woman – man's property or God's?

It is easy to get the impression that God made man first and woman as an afterthought, as if Adam told God he was lonely and so God got busy. However, it was always God's intention to make a helper for Adam. One who would stand side by side with him. Equal with him in every way. Woman was part of God's eternal design. It was planned. It was prepared. It was predestined that Eve would come out of Adam's side – in the image of God. So she was not Adam's property, she was God's property. Every woman, single or married, is stamped with the words, 'God's property. No trespassing.'

A healthy relationship in the family home makes for a healthy relationship in the marital home. So, fellas, look at how she gets on with her father. Do they have an affectionate relationship? Perhaps there's no father in the home. How does she relate to her brothers? Does she make you wait an hour for her in the living room (I mean, every time)? Does she try to keep up her health? If she gets sick after marriage, that's another thing. Then you stick it out. 'In sickness and in health. Till death do us part.'

Ladies, when you go to his home, keep your eyes open. Be as

1 CORINTHIANS 13

LOVE

If I speak with the eloquence of men and of angels, but have no love, I become no more than blaring brass or crashing cymbal. If I have the gift of foretelling the future and hold in my mind not only all human knowledge but the very secrets of God, and if I also have that absolute faith which can move mountains, but have no love, I achieve precisely nothing.

This love of which I speak is slow to lose patience – it looks for a way of being constructive. It is not possessive: it is not anxious to impress nor does it cherish inflated ideas of its own importance.

Love has good manners. It does not pursue selfish advantage. It is not touchy. It does not harbour grudges or gloat over the faults of others. On the contrary, it is glad when harmony and unity prevails.

Love knows no limit to its endurance, no end to its trust, no fading of its hope: it can outlast anything. It is, in fact, the one thing that still stands when all else has fallen.

Someone may have the spiritual gift of prophecy, but prophecies will be fulfilled and done with; someone may have the spiritual gift of speaking in tongues, but the need for them will one day disappear; another may have the spiritual gift of knowledge but it will one day be swallowed up in truth. All spiritual gifts will one day be superseded – all, that is, except love.

When I was a little child I talked and felt and thought like a little child. Now that I am grown up my childish speech and feeling and thought have no further significance for me.

Yet in some way we are still as little children. For at present all we see is the baffling reflection of reality. Some things just don't seem to make sense at all. The time will come, however, when we shall see reality whole and face to face! At present all I know is a little fraction of the truth, but the time will come when I shall know it as fully as God now knows me!

In this life we have three great lasting qualities – faith, hope and love. But the *greatest*; the **greatest** – the ***greatest*** of them all: is love.

ADAPTED FROM THE J. B. PHILLIPS PARAPHRASE, *LETTERS TO YOUNG CHURCHES*

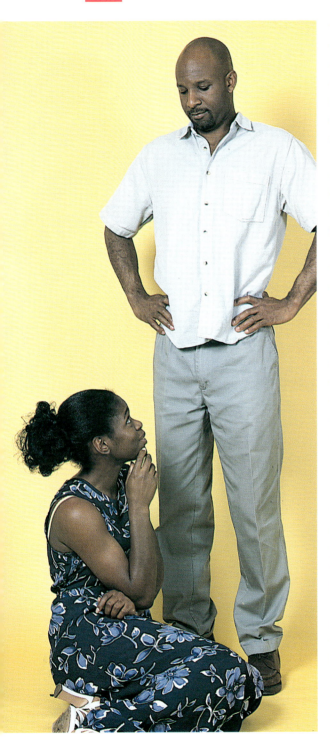

vigilant as the FBI. This thing called marriage is for life! How does he treat his mum? Is he tender and loving, or rude and demanding? Watch how that young man talks to you before you get married. Watch his behaviour, too. Is he on time for dates? Does he respect you? Does he hit you? If he hits you now, just wait till you get married! Some guys think that just because they buy you a burger and some cheap french fries they own you and can do anything they want with you, including premarital sex. He says, 'If you love me, you'll let me.' Just tell him, 'If you love me, you'll wait.' Many who've engaged in premarital sex will tell you that it did not strengthen the relationship as they had expected it would. Save close physical intimacy until marriage.

Is love all you need?
It is the great mystery of human love that makes two hearts beat as one. If love's all you've got, though, you're in trouble. The Beatles sang, 'All you need is love.' I've got news for you. Love is *not* all you need. You hear it all the time in premarital counselling: 'I know we've got these things against us, but we'll make it, because we're in love.'

In both Britain and America they publish an annual entitled,

> 'The whole concept of love is so distorted – and perverted – in our society, that it is difficult for people to get a proper basis for a marital relationship. As a marriage counsellor I often see people who assume that since they are no longer "high" – they are no longer in love. I usually tell my students that love is a very poor basis on which to get married. If all you've got going for you is that you're in love – then you need to terminate the relationship. I think it takes a lot more than love on which to build a marriage. You need loyalty, commitment, money, and on and on.'
> DR WALLACE DENTON

Who's Who? As long as you have excelled at something, whether you're a sports person or a college student, you can be on some list in *Who's Who?* Well, Sam Levenson wrote a book and called it, *You Don't Have to be in Who's Who to Know What's What*. I like that. In it he said: 'Love at first sight is easy to understand. It's when two persons have been looking at each other for years that it becomes a miracle.'

They talked to engaged couples in England and 40 per cent of them said they did not expect their forthcoming marriage to last. Forty per cent! Couples are no longer sure how long their marriage will last. That is because they have stopped saying, 'As long as *life* shall last,' and now they say, 'As long as *love* shall last.'

The truth is, this thing called marriage is too big for us to handle all by ourselves. If you're used to praying twice a day, double up on your prayers. Genesis 2:18 lets us know that God gave Adam a companion. *God* found a partner for Adam; and God is still in the business of finding partners today.

LOVE IS THE KEY

Ahead of the couple in love are a whole lot of locked doors. They are doors of mystery, ignorance, and uncertainty. These doors prevent you from seeing the real person you are marrying. You may think you know that person before you get married – but just wait a few months and you'll see! I have some keys to give you. I don't know what lies beyond. I don't know the nature of your potential or present barriers. I don't know what kind of locks are on the doors that confront you. But I *do* know about the power of these keys. If you will just remember to use them they will make all the difference in your life.

There are just three.
The first key is:

Love your partner
The apostle Paul says, 'Honour Christ by submitting to each other.'

'The grass is always greener on the other side of the fence' is a cliché. Look at, live for, invest in, and submit to *your* spouse. Tell her, tell him repeatedly, 'I love *you*.'

Love your partner. This idea of comparing your partner with someone else's partner ought to stop before it starts. If Mary's husband is so much better than yours then you should have married him. Somebody said, 'Ask for what you want and live with what you get.' You're there praising her husband, and his wife is there praising your husband, and neither of you can see the private faults so conveniently hidden in public. Look at *your* partner. Love *your* partner. Be thankful for what you've got. The word 'submit' is not a popular one today – even for people who love each other. Paul gives this definition of submission. He says, 'Love each other with brotherly affection. And take delight in honouring each other.' Submission means putting each other's happiness first. It means swallowing your pride. It may even mean changing your vocabulary.

There are certain words we have no problem saying before we are married. Words like 'Darling', 'Baby', 'Sweetheart', 'Sugar Dumpling'. Ah, but *after* you marry . . . . The sugar turns to salt. Sweet milk becomes sour cream. And if you're not careful, he starts to call you dumpling and leaves out the sugar . . . .

Talk is cheap – anybody can talk. Some men talk sweet roses but

Figuratively speaking, the man who has given red roses to his wife during courtship and the 'honeymoon phase' of early marriage, may begin to give her weeds soon afterwards. This is the first crisis in a marriage.

they deliver weeds. Somebody said, 'The man who talks by the mile and thinks by the inch, ought to be kicked by the foot.' I say, love your partner.

The second key is:

Love yourself
Take care of yourself. The apostle Paul says, 'That is how husbands should treat their wives, loving them as parts of themselves. No one hates his own body but lovingly cares for it, just as Christ cares for his body.' (Ephesians 5:28, 29, LB.)

I say, take care of yourself. Don't be so intent on looking out for him that you forget to look after yourself. Don't be so concerned with what he will think of the dinner. For while you are in the kitchen – in apron and curlers – wondering what he'll think of what you have done to the dinner, he's looking at what the dinner's done to you! *Look after yourself.*

Continue to desire to be physically attractive to each other – *in the house.* Men, this idea of dressing up to go to work but in the

home going around as if you have no comb, no razor, your face like a scouring pad . . . . No, look after the outside! Even more importantly, however, take care of the inside. Love who you are.

God has made you different – unique – special. Do not try to be somebody else. Just have a healthy appreciation for who *you* are. Loving yourself does not mean you've got no home repairs to do. It does mean, however, that you can accept yourself as you are because Christ accepts you as you are. All the while you are striving to reach God's ideal. There must be a commitment to growth. You should be able to say: 'I'm not what I want to be. I'm not what I'm going to be. But thank God I'm not what I was!' Love yourself.

The third and final key is:

Love your God
The apostle Paul again: 'Last of all I want to remind you that your strength must come from the Lord's mighty power within you. Pray all the time.' People marry in churches for a variety of reasons and that's their choice. But wherever the wedding takes place, having Christ as part of your *marriage* is not just an optional extra. It is vital if you want the marriage to succeed.

You see, love is not a two-way affair, it is a three-way relationship: a man, a woman and God. So that when a couple hits those locked doors marked 'Incompatibility', 'Communication Breakdown', and 'No More Love'; when the partners cannot bear to look at one another – they both look at God. And hey – guess what? – they find they're looking at each other!

Even if the feelings are not there. . . . I'm very serious now. Even if you think the spark is out forever. You do not like him anymore. You do not like her anymore. You can still *love* him. You can still *love* her. You can still commit yourselves to each other for better or for worse. Till death us do part. Why? Because our Lord and Master loved us when it was impossible for Him to like us. And that love cost Him His life. If Jesus is your Master, then you hold in your hand the key to marital happiness.

The Master Key
One day I was in church with an engaged couple. We were going to a room where we could counsel together and I was handed a bunch of keys. I enquired which key would fit the door. The answer came back, 'This one may. Or that one may. But *this* one definitely will. You see, this is the *master key*. It will open any door.'

So don't be afraid of the future.

Don't give up on each other when you come to those locked doors that threaten to mar your marital bliss. Take out your three keys. Try the one marked, *Love Your Partner;* it may get you through. Or try the one marked, *Love Yourself;* that may get you through. But if the way ahead is still blocked, then don't forget Jesus, your Master. ***Love Your God***. This is the *Master Key* – it will open any door.

There is a power for stability and maturing love within a marriage of which many couples do not avail themselves. It's called prayer.

LOVEWORK ON CHAPTER 2

BALANCING YOUR TRIANGLE

1 Examine the triangles below for a few minutes.
2 Which of the three sides needs more work right now?
3 Discuss your answers together.

NONLOVE

Lacking intimacy, passion or commitment
Casual interactions, for example, at the bank or supermarket, on the bus or train.

ROMANTIC LOVE

Intimacy and passion, lacking commitment
Intense involvement both verbally and physically but only for a short while, for example, a summer fling or a marriage soon in trouble.

LIKING

Intimacy, lacking passion and commitment
Not physical intimacy, but emotional, the ability just to talk together and enjoy it, for example, true friendship.

FATUOUS LOVE

Passion and commitment, lacking intimacy
Plenty of physical contact and promises to stay together (probably after knowing the person for a month), but lacking the emotional core necessary to sustain the relationship.

INFATUATION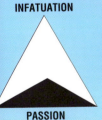

Passion, lacking intimacy and commitment
Plenty of physical contact, touching and love play, for example, love at first sight.

COMPANIONATE LOVE

Intimacy and commitment, lacking passion
Long-term friendship, for example, marriages where physical attraction has died down (or may never have been there at all).

EMPTY LOVE

Commitment, lacking intimacy and passion
Hanging in there through thick and thin, for example, thirty-year-old stagnant relationship.

CONSUMMATE LOVE

Intimacy, passion and commitment
When it all comes together and seems nicely balanced; and in case you hadn't noticed, you won't always be balanced.

The burdens and blessings of singleness

'We are not all the same. God gives some the gift of a husband or wife, and others he gives the gift of being able to stay happily unmarried.'
1 CORINTHIANS 7:7, LB.

Most of us will spend a significant part of our adult lives as single people. Our state of singleness may be temporary or it may be permanent. There are different categories of single people. They may be characterized by the four Ds and two Ss that follow.

Death. Death is often unexpected and leaves millions single and unprepared for it. Those single because of death are widows and widowers.

Divorce. Divorce and separation are also traumatic occurrences, sometimes even more traumatic than death.

Decision. There are those who have chosen by an act of the will to remain single, perhaps for religious reasons.

Delay. This accounts for the majority of singles and is an acute problem for many Christian women today. They are presently single but hope to marry one day. On every side one hears the cry, 'Where are the men?' On the one hand there is active delay. This is when a person postpones marriage in order to pursue a career or

> **DIVORCE CAN BE BOTH PAINFUL AND SUDDEN**
>
> Consider the case of Bill, a minister.
> It was a normal mid-March day. As I returned home from the church office for lunch, little did I realize that my life was about to fall apart. Lunch over, there was a knock on the door. A stranger asked in a cold monotone voice for William Scott Field. 'That's me,' I said. Immediately the visitor served papers requiring me to appear in family court on 30 March. My wife had sued for divorce. She wanted my home, my precious children, child support, alimony – and me out.
> I went into shock. In a few seconds my world fell apart. My pre-teen children were so close to me that the thought of leaving them pierced my soul. *MINISTRY*, JULY 1997, PAGE 22.

There are many reasons why some opt for – or settle for – the single life. One is an all-absorbing career. . . .

headed by a lone mother. The number of single parents increased from 150,000 in 1979 to 1.3 million in 1994. Many single parents are that way because of circumstances, but an increasing number have now been designated SMC – Single Mothers by Choice. One of every three lone parents has never married.

Spiritually single. These are people who are in fact married, but the one to whom they are married achieve an educational goal. Then on the other hand you have passive delay. This is when Mr or Mrs Right has not come along yet.

Single parents. In Britain more than one in six families are now

---

One girl's wedding day prayer illustrates the predicament of the spiritually single

'Dear God, I can hardly believe that this is my wedding day. I know I haven't been able to spend much time with You lately with all the rush of getting ready for today – and I'm sorry.

'I guess, too, I feel a little guilty when I try to pray about all this since Mark still isn't a Christian. But, oh, Father, I love him so much. What else can I do? I just couldn't give him up. Oh, You *must* save him, some way, somehow. You know how much I've prayed for him, and the way we've discussed the Gospel together. I've tried not to appear too religious, I know, but that's because I didn't want to scare him off. Yet he isn't antagonistic, and I don't understand why he hasn't responded. Oh, if only he were a Christian.

'Dear Father, please bless our marriage. I don't want to disobey You, but I do love him and want to be his wife. So please be with us, and please don't spoil my wedding day.'

does not share their faith. Often the effects of this are greater than could have been imagined.

Raymond Woolsey states:

'If there is not harmony on the basic level between religion and the marriage, one or the other or both – will suffer . . . . Such things as religious offerings, church attendance, family worship, may cause deep friction in a divided home.' *(Planning the Ideal Home,* page 30.)

The inability to share together spiritually is for some more acute than not being able to share sexually.

Let's examine the situation of singles in greater detail.

SELF-ESTEEM

The **S** of single stands for *self-esteem*. The full credentials of adulthood tend to be withheld from singles. Frequently they are viewed, and treated, as being in some way immature. One day it is hoped they will 'settle down' and get married. Unfit somehow because of their singleness, they are often kept from responsible positions at work or even in church, which a married person, even though younger, may fill. Single

The fact that one partner is unprepared to share spiritually, can be more devastating to a marriage than if a partner is unprepared to share sexually.

people may come to view themselves as less than complete.

Half a couple?
Some time ago we received a wedding invitation. It said, 'We are two halves becoming one . . . .' I smiled. Romantic, I thought, but is it true? Are we halves before we get married? I think of the person who said, 'Before I got married I was incomplete. After I got married I was totally finished.' But does the Bible state that wholeness is only found when a person says 'I do'? The Bible does not say two halves shall become one, but rather, ' "The two shall become one – no longer two, but one" ' (Matthew 19:5, LB). Two whole people becoming one whole couple.

Mathematics teaches us that one plus one equals two, but in biblical arithmetic, with the Father, Son, and Holy Spirit there to bless every Christian wedding, that mathematics becomes three plus two equals one. The unity we experience after marriage does not render our life before marriage fragmented, broken and dysfunctional. One *is* a whole number! When full personhood is denied, self-esteem must suffer. In many societies you find the notion that a woman is worthless without a husband. In some countries, once the woman has passed the age of 28 and is not married she is disregarded as a potential wife, being considered 'over the hill'.

Depression
Even in Western countries many feel they can only achieve full

One *is* a whole number! Singleness *is* a viable option!

identity when they have a partner. Psychologist Penelope Russianoff states, 'About 95 per cent of my female patients think that they are nothing without a man. The enormous desire for a male partner is probably the closest thing to a common denominator that women have.' As a consequence, single people are prone to depression. They may even turn to addictive behaviour to cover their unhappiness. Research published by Market Assessment Publications shows that single men and women drink more alcohol than married people, smoke more cigarettes, and have a greater risk of suffering cancer or heart disease. Depression from singleness can even lead to suicide. The number of young men in Britain killing themselves increased by 50 per cent between 1972 and 1989.

According to the experts, the flip side of singleness is that single people are more prone to alcohol abuse, more likely to be smokers, and have a greater risk of suffering cancer or heart disease.

Jesus gives value
The Christian's self-worth can never be based upon what people think about us or even what we think about ourselves. It is based upon what God thinks about us. Our value to God is not dependent on our age, race, class, nationality, gender, ability, or marital status, it is calculated by the price Jesus was willing to pay for our salvation, which was His life. Ellen White says, 'The Lord is disappointed when His people place a low estimate upon themselves. He desires His chosen heritage to value themselves according to the price He has placed upon them.' Single Christian women and men can hold up their heads and declare, 'I can value myself because Jesus values me.'

INTIMACY

The **I** of single stands for *intimacy*, an area of great concern for single people. Let us first look at the issue of sex education.

Sex education

This gets a bad press in many circles. Some think that sex education will lead to increased experimentation. Many are now acknowledging that it should be part of a *love education* curriculum. Tony Campolo says: 'A curriculum based on love rather than sex would work and, therefore, belongs in our schools. With sex ed, we show them how to do it, then we warn them not to do it – but we tell them if they decide to do it, to be careful, because it could kill them, make them sick, or produce an unwanted baby. Talk about confusion!'

When such a curriculum has been in place you can see the difference.

In South Africa, of the teenage girls who received sex education with a holistic perspective from home, school and church, 7 out of 10 decided to wait for marriage before having sexual intercourse. The remaining three decided to use contraceptives and one became pregnant. Of the teenage girls who received no information from home, school, or church, 6 out of 10 became pregnant.

God's plan

There is a divine triangle found in Genesis 2:24 which gives us insight into God's will for us: 'Therefore shall a man leave his father and his mother, and shall cleave unto his wife: and they shall be one flesh.' (KJV.) The Hebrew word used for leaving has as one of its meanings *to permit*. Two ideas are conveyed here. The first is that a person has now reached a certain maturity whereby he or she can be called an adult. Secondly, the man has to get permission of the parents to unite himself with their daughter as his wife. This 'uniting', or 'cleaving', implies commitment since the Hebrew word translated 'unity' or 'cleaving' means *to cling* or *to keep fast*. This word is used in the Bible not only with regard to marriage but also with the commitment we have towards God.

The Hebrew word for one flesh means *body*, indicating that the couple become one body. Many think this is simply the act of sex. Far more is intended here, however. The word not only refers to the physical body but the individual as a whole: physically, mentally and spiritually. The couple in marriage become one in purpose, mind and character, while remaining as two individuals. The distinct personalities of each partner still remain intact.

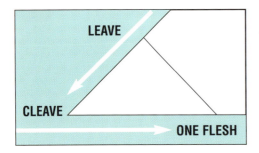

The sequence is from leave to cleave to one flesh. Notice there is no arrow directly from leave to one flesh. It is God's intention that sexual intercourse take place within the security of a committed marital relationship.

Cohabitation

Cohabitation is defined as a relationship in which a man and a woman live together and regularly engage in sexual intercourse without being married. Some people think that they can leave, cleave, and achieve a one-flesh relationship by just living together without being married. There has been a dramatic rise in cohabitation in recent years.

In the mid-60s in Britain around 5 per cent of single women lived with their future husband before marriage. By the 1990s about 70 per cent were cohabiting prior to marriage. Of women marrying a second time in the 1990s, about 90 per cent will cohabit before their second marriage. Why do people

want to cohabit? Three main reasons: striving for independence, testing the compatibility of a partner, or as a substitute for marriage. Many couples choose cohabitation as a permanent alternative to marriage, but most plan to marry in the future, 'when the time is right'. So what's wrong with trial marriage?

Trial marriage
'I'm not against marriage, but if it's not going to work out I want to know before I get into it.' Many people express this view today. 'We'll just test the waters, test our compatibility and commitment. If the spark's not there we'll just quit and move on without the hassle of divorce.' The statistics, however, give the real picture: *couples who cohabit before marriage are twice as likely to divorce.* The idea that living together before marriage reduces your chances of divorce is a lie. What is it that cohabiting couples miss out on?

The Bible tells us it's fine to be single and it's fine to be married. It's also fine to be engaged, but since marriage is not a game, don't play pretend marriage. In Christian marriage you state publicly before your community that you are making a love commitment to one person for as long as you shall live, a commitment that is binding for better or for worse, in

sickness and in health. Christians enter into a covenant with God, their spouse and their community to stay and grow together through the good times and the bad.

Such a commitment recognizes that my husband will not always look as good as he does now. My wife won't always have her shapely figure. There are other attractive people in the world, and chances are I'll bump into some of them. But, God helping me, I will forsake all others and keep myself only for my spouse. As a single person, by reserving sex until marriage, you can start being faithful to your potential marriage partner right now.

In the area of intimacy, there are no easy answers for the single person because God has made us as sexual beings. Dr Keith Burton, in his book *We Have Come this Far by Faith,* cries out, 'Let's get real and start acting like *real* men who are able to take responsibility for our own actions. For too long it has been the onus of the woman to say "no". However, a real man will be able to exercise the kind of self-restraint it takes to allow our women to remain ladies.' You don't have to discover your sexual compatibility before you get married. AIDS will tell you, there are bigger things to worry about. It may be a struggle to control yourself until marriage, but it's worth it. You may have noticed that most worthwhile things come with a struggle.

NEEDS
The **N** of single stands for *needs*.

> 'God has confidence in you, a human being whom He has created with a capacity for self-control much higher than he gave animals. Animals cannot wait for anything. They gratify their desires immediately. Have you ever watched a dog or a he-goat when they are under intense sexual pressure? They cannot wait for the appropriate time and place. Your dog will do it whenever and wherever the drive finds it, as long as there is a female nearby. Surely you can do better than this? Human beings are able to wait they can at least wait until they reach their bedroom, or until nobody is looking. Now consider this: if you can wait for an hour until the timing or the place is appropriate, then you can control yourself. Just exploit the same power of self-control to wait till the appropriate time; and that is: until you will be doing it with your spouse. Does it pay to wait? If it does, is it worth it? If it is, then wait!'

The following concerns have been raised by single people.
Numbering 1 to 20, which would concern you most?
How can you now start to work on your concerns?

CONCERNS

- ☐ Communication and listening
- ☐ Finances
- ☐ Self-worth and individuality
- ☐ Personal attractiveness
- ☐ Worship and spiritual growth
- ☐ Sexuality
- ☐ Establishing values and priorities
- ☐ Dealing with anger and irritation
- ☐ Sensitivity to others' needs/feelings
- ☐ Singles' relationship to the church
- ☐ Problems of the single parent
- ☐ Loneliness
- ☐ Coping with grief
- ☐ Stigma of divorce
- ☐ Pressure to marry or remarry
- ☐ Handling rejection
- ☐ Single social life
- ☐ Dating and remating
- ☐ Handling holidays
- ☐ Getting older as a single

GOD
The **G** of single stands for *God*. When God began His creation of humankind He first created Adam, a single person.

What's 'not good' about being single?
In Genesis 2:18 the Bible says, 'It is not good that the man should be alone.' (KJV.) What God did not say was, 'It is not good that man should be single.' Single people have the ability to form friendships and so need not be alone. There is a difference between alone and single. God made man first for relationship with Himself, and then with each other. God's first priority is that we should be complete in Him (Colossians 2:10). There are, after all, some benefits in being single.

Firstly, *your time is your own*. You don't have to tell anyone when you'll be home in the evening! You are free to develop your potential, pursue your interests, take advantage of spur-of-the-moment opportunities. You can devote a year of your life in volunteer mission service as thousands, in fact, have done. You can do simple things like spending an hour listening to a friend.

Secondly, *your money is your own*. Many say, 'Two can live as cheaply as one', but they usually say that before they get married.

Pattiejean couldn't believe how free she was to step out of her office in Bermuda and buy a dress if it caught her eye. Now a dress has to catch her eye, and my eye, her pocket and my pocket!

Through Christ, singleness is transformed from a problem to a gift (Matthew 19:22; 1 Corinthians 7:7); and James 1:17 teaches that all God's gifts are good, even perfect. So being single is not God's second best. It is a gift from God and God doesn't give second-rate gifts.

In Jesus there is no male or female, young or old, black or white, single or married, in the sense that one is more approved or accepted or important (Galatians 3:28). If singleness is one of the gifts God has chosen to allow us at this particular time in our lives, as God's stewards it is our duty to make the most of it, not as something done grudgingly, but happily and creatively.

LONELINESS
The **L** of single stands for *loneliness*. Loneliness is a feeling common to married people when distance or circumstance temporarily separates spouse from spouse. But while loneliness is part of the human condition, it is more often acutely felt by singles. There is no-

body around to jostle with, throw ideas around with; that somebody who will constantly act as sandpaper, smoothing and refining us. We become preoccupied with our singleness and feeling of incompleteness. We get skin hunger – no one to touch, and some of us live in societies where physical contact so often has sexual overtones.

It's difficult handling the pressure to marry or remarry so often put on singles by well-meaning friends. It's hard staying calm, cool and collected when they are rude, thoughtless and ignorant. You may be single, but you don't have to be constantly lonely. You can live as a happy, fulfilled single person if you will bear in mind the following five points:

❏ *Don't link singleness with ugliness.* If you find yourself saying, 'What's wrong with me, no one seems to want me for a spouse, I really must be ugly', then think of the friends that you have. You are not ugly to them. The fact that you are single often has more to do with circumstances than how physically desirable you are.

❏ *Maintain a large circle of friends.* Don't do it with marriage in mind, but recognize that having other people around you will give you insights into your own self. People are like windows and it is possible that without them around we

> *It's evening, Lord,*
> *And I feel the peace of solitude.*
> *I am alone tonight, as every night.*
> *But I am not lonely.*
> *I praise You*
> *for the gentleness of these quiet hours.*
> *I thank You*
> *for the gift of faith —*
> *faith that assures me*
> *that You have not forgotten me tonight*
> *and that You*
> *will often remember me*
> *with showers of peace*
> *like these that fall just now.*
>
> SHOWERS OF PEACE, by Ann Elise Burke

would not achieve our full potential.

❏ *Consider moving.* Now if you have a strong sense of calling to your work location or the place where you live, by all means stay. But if friends of your own age, status and convictions are in short supply, then move on!

❏ *Decide the sex issue.* Realize that the single Christian who these days believes in chastity before marriage takes a daring stand. God intends sex to be infinitely more than a casual sport. He intends it to achieve its greatest beauty and fulfilment in the loving, caring, committed relationship of marriage. Make a decision on this issue calmly and thoughtfully when emotions and temptations are not strong. You've got to decide that you're going to treat your body as the temple of God.

GOD'S PLAN FOR SEX

'To sum it up, my brothers, we beg and pray you by the Lord Jesus, that you continue to learn more and more of the life that pleases God, the sort of life we told you about before. You will remember the instructions we gave you then in the name of the Lord Jesus. God's plan is to make you holy, and that entails first of all a clean cut with sexual immorality. Every one of you should learn to control his body, keeping it pure and treating it with respect, and never regarding it as an instrument for self-gratification, as do pagans with no knowledge of God. You cannot break this rule without in some way cheating your fellow-men. And you must remember that God will punish all who do offend in this matter, and we have warned you how we have seen this work out in our experience of life. The calling of God is not to impurity but to the most thorough purity, and anyone who makes light of the matter is not making light of a man's ruling but of God's command. It is not for nothing that the Spirit God gives us is called the *Holy* Spirit.'

1 THESSALONIANS 4:1-8, JBP.

❏ *Live for Jesus.* You've got to come to the place where you believe that it's just not worth living any other way than to live for Jesus. No matter how rich or successful or famous or married it is, no other life will satisfy our needs.

EXPECTATIONS

The **E** of single stands for *expectations*. What can a single person expect from the future? We may not know what the future holds but we know who holds the future. Our job is simply to trust our Maker. When the apostle Paul considered his condition he declared:

'I have learned to be content, whatever the circumstances may be. I know now how to live when things are difficult and I know how to live when things are prosperous. In general and in particular I have learned the secret of facing either poverty or plenty. I am ready for anything through the strength of the one who lives within me.' (Philippians 4:11-13, JBP.)

So I leave you with three special words. The first is *rejoice*.

Rejoice

Don't spend your time wondering why you have missed the best.

ON HIS PLAN FOR YOUR LIFE

Everyone longs to give himself to someone – to have a deep soul relationship with another . . . to be loved thoroughly and exclusively. But to the Christian, God says, 'No, not yet; not until you are satisfied and fulfilled and content with being loved by me alone; with giving yourself totally and unreservedly to me – to having an intensely personal and unique relationship with me alone.

'I love you, my child, and until you discover that your satisfaction is to be found only in me, you will not be capable of the perfect human relationship I have planned for you. You will not be unified with each other until you are united with me exclusively. I want you to stop; stop wishing, stop planning and allow me to give you the most thrilling plan in existence, the one that you can't imagine.

'I want you to have the best. Please allow me to bring it to you . . . just keep watching me; expecting the greatest things. Keep expecting that satisfaction, knowing that I am. Don't be anxious. Don't worry. Don't look around at the things you think you want. You just keep looking away and up to me, or you'll miss what I have to show you.

'Then, when you're ready, I'll surprise you with love more exciting and wonderful than any you could ever dream of. You see, until you're ready – I'm working this minute to have you both ready at the same time – until you are both ready, you won't be able to experience the love that amplifies your relationship with me, and to enjoy the everlasting union of beauty and perfection and love I offer you with myself.

'KNOW THAT I LOVE YOU UTTERLY. I AM GOD ALMIGHTY. BELIEVE ME AND BE SATISFIED.'

Singleness can mean more opportunities to be of service to others.

Whether you have never been married or you are divorced or widowed, you can learn to lead a happy, full, and satisfying life as a single person. Don't cherish some lost moment of the past or chase some elusive dream of the future. Go places, do things, enjoy people. Pursue your interests. Don't be afraid to do things alone, if need be. Enjoy life now. Secondly, *reverse*.

Reverse
Make a 180-degree turn and say to yourself, 'I will stop searching for the "one and only", knowing that as I become more free to be myself I will be freer to care about others. I will, in my deepest feelings, know that it is all right to be single. No, it's more than all right, it's a marvellous opportunity to develop and use the gifts and abilities that God has given specifically to me.' Thirdly, *relax*.

Relax
Accept yourself. Discover yourself. List your strengths, liabilities, goals and interests. Work on the areas that you need to, but what you can't change, just accept! And remember, God is still in the business of finding partners. Give Him control of your life, believing that 'all that happens to us is working for our good if we love God and are fitting into his plans'. (Romans 8:28, LB.)

LOVEWORK ON CHAPTER 3

Single, struggling, but still standing

Single person, take a week at the beginning of each month to read this singles' affirmation, just to remind your head what you know in your heart. Remember the words of Paul: 'I'm not saying you *must* marry; but you certainly *may* if you wish. . . . But we are not all the same. God gives some the gift of a husband or wife, and others he gives the gift of being able to stay happily unmarried.' (1 Corinthians 7:6, 7, LB.)

SUNDAY

I will have goals that are realistic but will nonetheless stretch me, knowing I will feel a sense of achievement and heightened self-esteem once the goal is accomplished, and, should marriage come, I will have much more to contribute to its richness and eventual success.

MONDAY

I won't neglect my devotional life. I will spend some time each day in prayer and Bible study.

TUESDAY

Instead of searching for the 'one and only' I will realize the tremendous importance of friendships and will develop worthwhile friends of both sexes.

WEDNESDAY

I will have an active social life, involving sports, cultural and church events.

THURSDAY

I will maintain a healthy attitude towards dating. There are good men/women out there. Just because I haven't found one doesn't mean that all men/women are bad.

FRIDAY

I will recognize that God's plan for sexual fulfilment is still the best – sexual release with one's partner, receiving pleasure through their pleasure. Though sexual control can be overbearing at times, I will not allow my sexual fulfilment to take place outside of a committed relationship of marriage, not with

Not only is it 'OK to be single', singleness provides great opportunities for friendship, personal growth and educational advancement.

just any partner – neither with myself.

SATURDAY

I will, in my deepest feelings, know that it's all right to be single and, becoming braver, know that it's even more than all right – it can be a great and untapped opportunity for continuous personal growth.

'My brothers (and sisters), I do not consider myself to have "arrived", spiritually, nor do I consider myself already perfect. But I keep going on, grasping ever more firmly that purpose for which Christ grasped me. My brothers, I do not consider myself to have fully grasped it even now. But I do concentrate on this: I leave the past behind and with hands outstretched to whatever lies ahead I go straight for the goal – my reward the honour of being called by God in Christ. All of us who are spiritually adult should set ourselves this sort of ambition, and if at present you cannot see this yet, you will find that this is the attitude which God is leading you to adopt.'
PHILIPPIANS 3:12-15 (JBP).

It takes two to submit

'For the office of a bishop a man must be of blameless reputation, he must be married to one wife only, and be a man of self-control and discretion. He must be a man of disciplined life. . . . He must have proper authority in his own household, and be able to control and command the respect of his children. (For if a man cannot rule in his own house how can he look after the Church of God?)'

'The willing subjection of the Church to Christ should be reproduced in the submission of wives to their husbands. But, remember, this means that the husband must give his wife the same sort of love that Christ gave to the Church, when he sacrificed himself for her.'

1 TIMOTHY 3:2-5 and EPHESIANS 5:24, 25, JBP.

You hear it all the time. Two men are talking. There's been a dispute at home. Husband and wife have not seen eye to eye. One man says to the other, 'Just tell her who wears the trousers in your house.'

Men today are attracted to women in the workplace. They appear confident, self-assertive, and composed. But in the home men often want women to be their property – their servants. Joyce Brothers said, 'Women want a husband who will consider them an equal partner. Not a kind of privileged domestic.' For many wives, home life is an unending drudgery. Somebody said it starts when you sink into his arms and ends with your arms in the sink!

Men and headship

In Ephesians 5:22 the apostle Paul says, 'Wives, submit yourselves to your husbands.' That's not at all popular today. Does it mean that you have to sit there and take abuse? Or irresponsibility? What about when he fails to get the car serviced? Or goes off playing golf when there's work to be done? Surely to accept *that* is to encourage it? Jesus had a different understanding of what it means to be the head.

The Bible has many definitions cf the word head. One of the meanings is origin or source. Christ is the head of the Church. No, he does not dominate the Church. He is the Source. He is the Origin. The Church came out of Christ. And because of that, Jesus loved it and

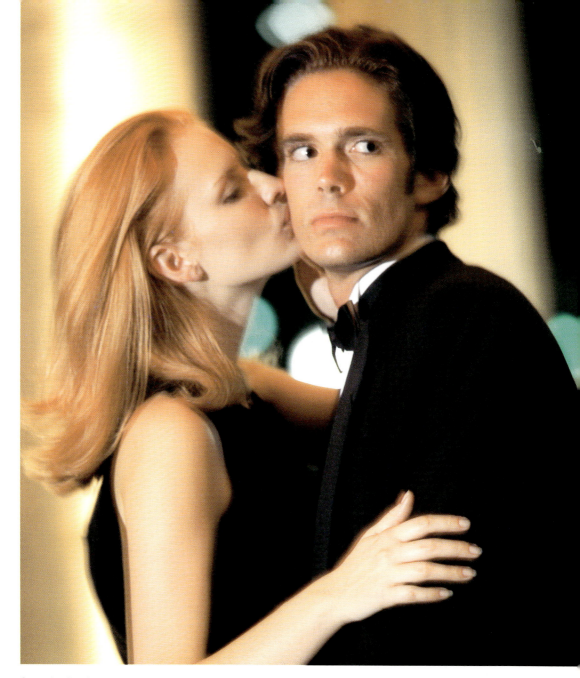

Some husbands try to have the best of both worlds – a submissive wife at home (to prepare the meals and mother the children) and a flirtation in the workplace. This leads to lies, hypocrisy and dereliction of responsibility, and, in the long term, hurt and endless problems.

gave Himself for it. The Bible says the husband is the head of the wife. No, he does not dominate. He is the source. The woman came out of man in the beginning. God took a rib out of Adam to fashion Eve.

Headship for the husband means selfless, sacrificial love. Submission for the wife means freely choosing to accept this

Christlike love. So submission, according to Scripture, is a submission not to the husband's wishes but to the husband's *love*. The husband's headship does not mean he's superior. And the wife's submission does not mean she's inferior.

Men and leadership
In fact, in Galatians 5:13 Christians, regardless of sex or status, are required to be 'servants of one another'. In Ephesians 5:21 the Bible says husbands and wives need to practise *mutual* submission. However, God expects the

Dear Dr Dobson

I have a problem and it has become a terrible burden to me. It is affecting me both physically and spiritually. I grew up in a good Christian home. But I married a man who was not a Christian. Paul and I have had a rough time. A lot of anger and fighting. He has refused to participate in the family as father of our three children. He leaves everything up to me. He likes to go bowling and watch football on TV – and he sleeps all Sunday. So things have always been rocky. But a much more serious problem arose.

Paul began to get interested in a beautiful divorcee. She works as his bookkeeper. At first it seemed innocent. But I began to notice our relationship was deteriorating. He always wanted this woman along whenever we went anywhere. And he spent more time at her house. He said they were doing accounting work. I didn't believe it. I began to nag and complain. It just made him more and more determined to be with her. Gradually, they fell in love with each other. I didn't know what to do about it.

I bought a book about this time. The author promised that if I'd obey my sinner husband, God wouldn't allow any wrong to happen. So long as I was submissive. Well, in my panic, I thought I would lose him forever. I agreed to let the other woman come into our bedroom with us. I thought it would make Paul love me more. But it just made him fall deeper in love with her.

Now he is confused. He doesn't know which one of us he wants. He doesn't want to lose me. He says he still loves me and our three kids. But he can't give her up either. I love Paul so dearly and I have begged him to turn our problem over to the Lord. I love the other woman too. I know she is also hurting. But she doesn't believe God will punish this sin. I have experienced terrible jealousy and pain. But I always put the needs of my husband and his friend above my own. But what do I do now? Please help me. I'm on the bottom looking up.
Signed Linda.
JAMES DOBSON, *LOVE MUST BE TOUGH*.

Too many men use romantic gestures to get the woman 'hooked', and then forget all about romance. They are the same men who are baffled when relationships disintegrate.

man to show a measure of initiative and a measure of leadership. H. Page Williams said, 'I often talk with men who say, "When my wife changes her attitude, then I'll change mine." But from God's point of view, men are to initiate love, and the male leader is to initiate reconciliation. It is not a matter of giving in, it's a matter of being honest and assuming the lead in your God-given responsibility.'

Men – sentimental or sensitive?
But we let other people shape our lives. You hear that if you want to be a man – I mean a real man – you can't be sentimental. Oh, yes, be romantic. You know, roses, chocolates, poetry. But that's just to get her hooked. After you've got her you can forget the romance and be a man. Make work your priority. Marriage must be secondary.

And what does being a man mean? Being tough. Macho. Don't

let feelings get to you. And never – I mean never – cry. Shed a tear once in a while, maybe. But never let her see it. Why? Because she'll think you are weak. *Oh, no, she won't. She'll think you are human, and she'll love you for it!* Pamela Wilson Culluson wrote an article called, 'Women's Rights and the Family'. In it she said:

'We must stop expecting men to live up to the rough-and-tough James Bond concept of masculinity. The existence of this unattainable concept fosters anxiety in men. It keeps them from expressing the human qualities of tenderness, compassion, humility, and co-operation.'

It's the shortest verse in the Bible. Just two words, but very powerful ones. John 11:35: 'Jesus wept.' *Jesus* wept. Jesus *wept*. He was touched. He broke down. It was all too much for Him. A sensible woman will understand a man's tears. She will not lose all respect for him. In fact, she will become closer to him than ever before.

Women and submission
'Do you think I am submissive to my husband?' That was a question Nancy van Pelt asked two hundred young college women during a seminar on preparing for marriage. She said they all had a good chuckle over their negative re-

If men want to succeed with relationships it is likely that they will have to modify certain aspects of what they perceive as the Macho Male image.

sponses. One said she was too tall to be submissive. Another said she talked too much to be submissive. That's *not* what submission is all about.

The Christian emphasis is not so much on the submissiveness of the wife, but on the radical change in behaviour expected of the husband. The two key concepts here are headship and submission. The Greek word 'head' (*kephale*) is used seventy-five times in the New Testament, but never in the sense

What does the Bible mean when it invites marriage partners to be 'submissive'?

of overpowering domination. Similarly, submission in marriage is not defined as subservience. *Kephale* may be used as a metaphor to mean 'source' or 'point of origin'. So Adam was the 'source' or 'point of origin' of Eve – she came out of him just as the Church came out of Christ (the head) – nothing to do with domination.

The husband does have the role of headship, but it is selfless, sacrificial and agapic love. Submission for a wife is to choose freely to accept this Christlike love. Submission, then, is not to the husband's *wishes* but to the husband's *love!* Thus the husband's headship does not signal superiority and the wife's submission does not indicate inferiority.

It's all the apostle Paul's fault
Paul was not attempting to put forward a law that would subjugate women; that existed already. No, Paul wanted to show the world something that was radically different from the contemporary customs and culture. The name of the game would no longer be control and get, it was now to be love and serve. Paul is extremely clever. He takes the contemporary term headship and radically transforms it. So, Christian husband, you can still say you are the head of the house, as your non-Christian neighbour says it, *but you don't mean the same thing*. What your neighbour means is that when he comes home his wife brings him his slippers. What *you* mean is when you wife comes home you bring her her slippers! So the traditional view of the male as the head of the family is preserved, but that *headship is a function only, not a matter of status or superiority*.

It takes two to submit
There is a verse that many men don't like to read. It's before the one that counsels wives to submit. This is what it says: 'Submitting yourselves one to another in the fear of God.' (Ephesians 5:21, KJV.) Paul is stressing the idea of mutual submission. Mutual submission requires that Christians, regardless of status, function, sex, or rank, 'through love be servants [literally "slaves"] of one another' (Galatians 5:13). If a partner is to submit as Christ's Church is to submit, then the biblical definition of submission is a free response and uncoerced surrender to the self-sacrificing, unconditional love of a compassionate and committed spouse.

Mutual submission is Christian and it's a beautiful thing. It combines respect with tough love. I believe that when people of the world look at a Christian home

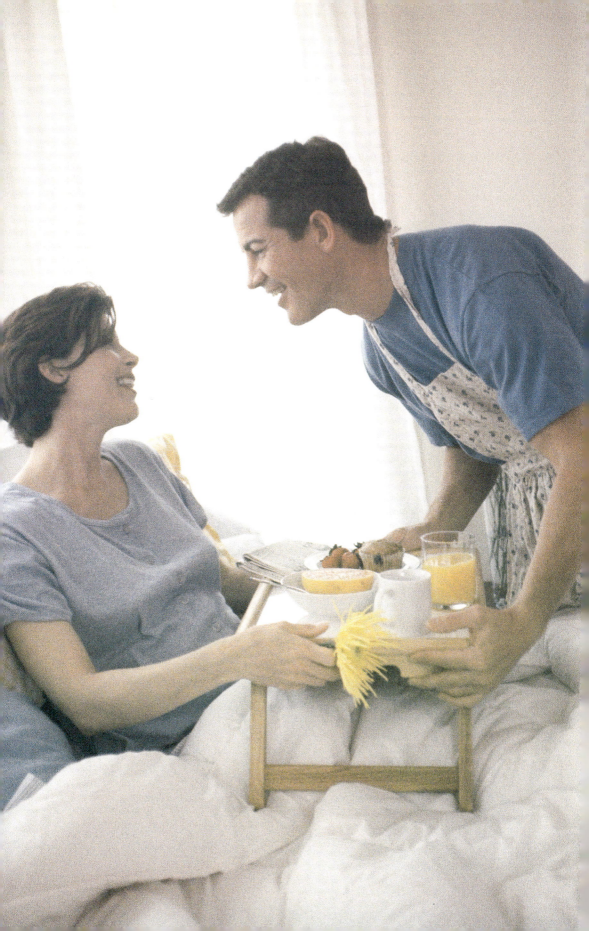

they have a right to see something different. A man and a woman not striving to be boss. Instead, they're striving to outdo one another in love. Nobody imposes his or her will on the other anymore. Nobody gives in just for the sake of peace. They seek God together. They develop together. They grow together. Christian marriage has been defined as a union of loving service to others.

Jesus said that worldlings lord it over their own, but it should not be so among you. And Philippians 2:3 tells us, 'With humility of mind let each of you regard one another as more important than himself.' That's what a Christian marriage ought to be like. Ephesians 5:25 says, 'Husbands, love your wives, just as *Christ* also loved the church.' (RAV.) If you want to know how to treat your wife, just look at how Jesus treated us. John 13:1 says, 'Having loved his own who were in the world, he loved them to the end.' (RAV.) Jesus poured out Himself in love for the Church. And to think that Jesus was the Head of the Church!

The purpose of Christian marriage is the discovery and carrying out of God's will in a relationship of acceptance and commitment. This acceptance is exalted beyond interpersonal dialogue and human intimacy. It is patterned on, and it reflects, the sacrificial relationship Christ Himself has with the Church. And make no mistake about it, it works.

Learning from each other
David and Vera Mace, pioneers of marriage enrichment, believe that cross-cultural understandings of mate selection will immeasurably strengthen marriage preparation as currently practised in the West. They state:
'In cultural values, in social institutions, even to some extent in political organizations, the East believes it has traditions that are better for its way of life than anything the West can offer. Certainly this is true of family life.'

Family systems
There are three recognized types of family system:

Firstly there is *monogamy*, where each person has one spouse.

There is *polygamy*, where there are multiple spouses. In polygamy you will find *polygyny,* where a man has more than one wife (for economic and political reasons, rather than sexual), and *polyandry*, where a woman has more than one husband. You will find polyandry in the Todas tribe of Southern India, for example, but it is very rare.

Thirdly, there is *group marriage*.

In group marriage, men and women have legal sexual access to each other. There is no society where this form of marriage is a predominant model, but it is practised by minority segments within a larger society.

There are four basic positions Christians have taken on the polygamy issue. Some have said that it is simply a sin, comparable with adultery; others have called it an inferior form of marriage, unacceptable for Christians. Others believe polygamy to be a form of marriage which cannot do justice to the full spirit of Christian marriage but which can be tolerated just as Christians have put up with slavery and dictatorial governments, for example. Still others consider polygamy one form of marriage and monogamy another.

Many people think of Africa when they hear the word polygamy, but it is a practice which is actually decreasing in Africa and increasing in America! Britain's *Sunday Times* reported on 11 January 1998:

'Polygamy has more practitioners in America today – an estimated 35,000, including many family members – than in the time of Brigham Young, the nineteenth-century Mormon leader who was reputed to have fathered fifty-six children with sixteen wives. Threats of "excommunication"

> **FOUR PATTERNS OF MATE SELECTION**
>
> ❏ Selection by the parents, where the young people themselves are not consulted.
> ❏ Selection by the parents, but the young are consulted.
> ❏ Selection by the young people, but parental approval is necessary.
> ❏ Selection by the young people, where the parents are not consulted.

Monogamy is the Bible model for marriage.

from the Church hierarchy have done little to dampen the growing passion for polygamy.'

When an unmarried person is converted to Christ, the biblical ideal of a one man and one woman relationship (Genesis 2:24) should be practised.

Serial monogamy
What tends to be more common all over the world today, in Europe and the Americas, Asia and Australasia, as well as in Africa and the Caribbean, is *serial monogamy*, namely, being 'sexually faithful' to one partner until that relationship ends. No matter how sophisticated this may sound, sexually-transmitted diseases will attack serial monogamists just as much as serial polygamists. The question was asked on an English language paper: 'A Christian should have only one wife – what is this called?' The student wrote, 'Monotony'. Laugh if you want, but God's plan will keep you both happy and alive.

Parental involvement
The intense feelings of youth should be balanced with the detached judgement of more mature experience. The ideal is a co-operative selection by young people and parents together. Where this is the case, a platform is laid for harmonious relations with in-laws. In many countries a dowry, or bride price, or *labola,* is paid, sometimes in cattle, sometimes in cash. The system has worked well in some cases, but it is often abused, resulting in great misery. Women are often in conflict with their spouses and their mothers-in-law, who may reside with them. It is to in-law relations that we now turn.

In-laws
One mother said, 'When my daughter married, I made a vow that I'd let her live her own life, even if I had to show her how to do it.' In-laws or out-laws? I want you to know today that when you get married you don't just marry *into* a family, you marry a family!

If the in-law crisis doesn't hit before the wedding, it is likely to reach its peak soon after. Parents have a hard time letting go of someone they've cared for for so long. And the extent to which you realize this will determine whether your relatives are in-laws or out-laws.

So we're having a quiz. Ten statements, true or false?

1 *'Generally mothers-in-law are problems.'*
That's **true**. Studies show that the husband's mother will most likely pose the biggest problem. The husband's mother probably identifies

more closely with the wife's role. Therefore she is likely to be very critical of how another woman is performing a role that she has successfully filled for years. Yes, generally, mothers-in-law are a problem. But then, generally, so are daughters-in-law! It takes at least two people to create an in-law problem. No one person is entirely to blame. You can't pin all the blame on the mother-in-law!

2 *'Fathers-in-law are as much a problem in most marriages as are mothers-in-law.'*
True. Mothers-in-law can cause trouble because of what they say. Fathers-in-law cause trouble because of what they don't say. Silence is not always golden. There are times when you have to put the newspaper down and actually take a stand. Your child's marriage may depend on it.

3 *'It is unwise to accept money from in-laws when first married.'*
This is a tough one. Knowing the pressures, I would say, **False;** accept the money. But take great care that you know what you are doing. Many counsellors will tell you not to accept.

Some studies have shown that couples argue over money more than anything else. It is closely linked with power. Because the Bible emphasizes the power of love over the love of power, it has much to say on the subject of finances. There are about five hundred verses in the Bible dealing with prayer, about five hundred verses on faith, but over two thousand verses in the Bible concerning

---

YOU BE THE COUNSELLOR

Mary and Dave seemed to have a great marriage. They had a small but tastefully-decorated flat. They both worked and were able to keep their heads above water. After about six years of marriage Mary stopped work because they were expecting their first child. It became a crisis. They would have to get a bigger place. They would be bringing home less money so they would have to ask Dave's father for help, and he agreed. Because he was a widower, Mary invited him to live with them. It was a mistake. You see, Dave and his father were in business partnership together.

Little by little their money blended into one fund. Dave and the father-in-law felt that Mary spent money foolishly, so she was given an allowance. With this she had to buy groceries, and pay the bills. You guessed it, the money couldn't stretch that far. She had to ask her husband and her father-in-law for more. There was nothing left over for her personal needs. Mary was discouraged, disheartened, and frustrated. What would you tell her to do?

Surveys indicate that couples are more likely to argue about financial priorities than about any other subject.

money and possessions. They are worth reading!

4 *'Usually a visit to the in-laws should be made at least once a year.'* Well, I don't think you'd want to put a hard-and-fast time on it, but you ought not to let a whole year pass while you are planning to go and see them and never making it. Looked at like that, I guess I'd put **True.** Be careful about making a trip to the in-laws your holiday.

Don't live with your parents. You can't develop intimacy with your spouse when you're living in somebody else's home. You may be reluctant to show physical affection during the day, or afraid of making a noise at night. Your sex life may be curtailed. Even if they offer you the whole upstairs, leave it alone.

5 *'It's wise to move away from in-laws so that the couple can begin their marriage without interference from their parents.'*

After what I have just said, I suppose you're expecting me to say, True. Well, the extended family can be a tremendous blessing to you, so I say, **False.** You don't necessarily have to leave town in order to keep your marriage alive. But some counsellors will say, True. Somebody said the best husband you can marry is the man who really loves his mother but lives five hundred miles away from her. Well, I don't know about that. But Genesis 2:24 has some relevant advice: 'For this reason a man will *leave* his father and mother and be united to his *wife*, and they will become one flesh.' (NIV, emphases ours.) Men, you've got to untie those apron strings, and women, if he doesn't have the guts to do it, you get a knife and cut him loose! For the sake of your marriage, men, learn to please your wife. Put her happiness before your own. If it means you've got to force yourself to love her apple crumble, so be it, but leave mother's crumble in mother's fridge. Put your spouse's interests before your own. Somebody has said the only difference between unite and untie is where you place the 'I'. Watch out for that 'I'.

6 *'In-laws can give security and intellectual guidance to newly-married couples.'*
True. Work at establishing a good relationship with your in-laws. In other words, make friends with them. Husbands, send a bouquet of flowers to your mother-in-law on her birthday. Wives, send his mum a thoughtful gift on Mother's day. Invite them to dinner sometimes, or take them out. It might cost a little but the rewards can be great. If you treat your in-laws like friends, they'll treat you the same way.

7 *'A daughter-in-law should honour her husband's parents by doing what her mother-in-law advises.'*
False. Read the Ten Commandments first. Exodus 20:12 says, 'Honour your father and your mother, so that you may live long in the land the Lord God is giving you.' (NIV.) Wives and husbands, be respectful; and husbands, protect your wife!

8 *'Mothers-in-law are a good source for child-rearing advice.'*
Unquestionably, **True.** It's always better, though, that you ask for

help, rather than mother-in-law dispensing it like food stamps. The apostle Paul says that the older women should, 'teach what is good. Then they can train the younger women to love their husbands and children.' (Titus 2:3, 4, NIV.) Don't worry, the men aren't getting off scot-free. The passage goes on to state that men, especially young men, need to practise strict self-control. They have got to be an example.

9 *'When first married it's wise to have some clear mutual expectations with in-laws.'*
True. There are questions that all parents-in-law-to-be should ask themselves, such as: When the newlyweds choose something that is not your choice, what do you think your response will be? What plans, secrets, and problems do you expect the new couple to share with you? If this does not happen, what do you think your reaction will be? Will you expect them to visit you often? How do you define 'often'? How will you go about suggesting they visit you? Do you expect the newly-married couple to call before visiting you and vice versa? Can these be spontaneous 'drop-ins'? Written responses to questions such as these can be shared with the couple during premarital counselling sessions.

10 *'The husband should take the initiative in solving problems when they're between his mother and his wife.'*
True. Guys, don't ask me why on this one, just trust me, the answer is true! It's probably because the husband is the link between the wife and the mother-in-law, and is loved and respected by both.

No matter how close the extended family, you've got to keep a sacred circle. There are some things which no one else has a right to know. And so, three 'nevers' to close:
– *never* discuss the faults of your mate with your parents;
– *never* quote your family or hold them up as models to your mate;
– *never* threaten to, or actually go home to mother.

In one study more than five hundred university student couples in their first years of marriage ranked in-law relationships at the top of a list of difficult areas of adjustment. Statistics show that in-law disagreements affect the early years of marriage more than any other problem. If the extended family is going to mean anything at all, it means you've got to think this thing out before, during and after the wedding day. It's going to take work, but the benefits are worth it. Tell yourself you're going to enjoy your new family – and you will.

Often early marriage conflicts are over in-law problems. The most pathetic figure is the married man who still accepts direction from his mother.

LOVEWORK ON CHAPTER 4

What would you like to do?

As a group of counsellors, we were discussing a client whose marriage was in jeopardy because the husband would regularly step over the milk containers which had been delivered to the doorstep and would rarely bring them inside. I thought it was laughable until one of the counsellors admitted that she was guilty of the same thing and it was a source of great irritation in their marriage.

In the following exercise be sure to fill in the frequency column, for example, annually, monthly, weekly, daily, etc. And feel free to add more tasks!

TASKS	FREQUENCY	HUSBAND	WIFE	OTHER
Car needs				
Vacuuming				
Budgeting				
Cooking				
Washing				
Washing up				
Dusting				
Tidying up				
Ironing				
Sewing				
Setting table				
Worship leader/ordering worship materials				
Paying school fees				
Paying credit card and utility bills on time				
Supervising children's homework				
Caring for pet's needs				
Mowing lawn				
Ensuring the garden has flowers not weeds				
Taking out the rubbish				
Maintaining medical records				
Keeping important documents (passports, etc.)				
Remembering to send out greetings cards				
Preparing tax returns, insurance, pension, etc.				
Bringing deliveries inside (milk, post, etc.)				

5 Twenty years, no argument. *Really?*

'We are not separate units but intimately related to each other in Christ. If you are angry, be sure that it is not out of wounded pride or bad temper. Never go to bed angry – don't give the devil that sort of foothold. . . . Let there be no more resentment, no more anger or temper, no more violent self-assertiveness, no more slander and no more malicious remarks. Be kind to each other, be understanding. Be as ready to forgive others as God for Christ's sake has forgiven you.'
EPHESIANS 4:25-27, 31, 32, JBP.

Who is the real you?

When a couple stand before the minister to get married there are more than just two people in front of him. There are six. Yes, that's right. There's the woman that *she* thinks she is. There's the woman that *he* thinks she is. And there's the woman that she *really* is. Then there's the man that *he* thinks he is. There's the man that *she* thinks he is. And there's the man that he *really* is. And love's task is to figure out who in the world you've got married to!

Many couples are shocked by the disagreements that they have, and interpret their quarrels as signs that their love has gone. Perhaps, they think, they made a mistake getting married in the first place. What couples need to recognize is that the person to whom they are now married is not the

How many people know – *really* know – the person they are marrying?

person they married. Changes have occurred. In actual fact, the person they now see may not have changed very much but now they are seeing their real character.

If there's one thing that turns people off, it's hearing a couple say: 'We've been married for twenty years, and we've never had an argument yet.' It has been said, 'When a married couple tell me they have a conflict-free relationship, I can tell you one of three things is true of them: either they are liars, one's an idiot, or the other is dead.' Strong marriages anticipate conflict *and remain committed through it all*.

Marks of a strong family
Lasswell and Lasswell studied 130 families which they considered to be strong, cohesive, and functional. While there were many differences among these families, there were six qualities which stood out.

❑ *Family members appreciated each other.*
Criticism was replaced by compliments; family members built one another up instead of tearing one another down.
❑ *Family members arranged their personal schedules so that they had time to be together as a family.*
Family togetherness was both spontaneous and planned.

❏ *Family members had positive communication patterns.*

These involved openness, honesty, patience, respect, concern, and a willingness to discuss differences. Family members listened to what the other person was saying and feeling.

❏ *Family members displayed a high level of commitment to their family.*

There was a high level of bonding, a sense of belonging, a willingness to invest time and energy into a team venture. There was a commitment to work for whatever growth and change was necessary for establishing a strong family.

❏ *Family members possessed a spiritual orientation.*

They were not all regular church attenders (though many were), but they had a strong value system or moral base upon which to build their lives.

❏ *Family members were able to deal positively with crises.*

They were able to face their problems realistically and creatively in such a way that crises pulled them together, not apart.

Are you a natural?

Many couples have the unrealistic expectation that anger and conflict should not exist in a loving relationship. A happy marriage is not defined by the absence of conflict, but by the possession of conflict-resolution skills. Couples need to acquire the techniques necessary to make creative use of anger and conflict. The companionship-style of marriage is built on equality and the acquisition of relational skills. Some people believe in the myth of naturalism, which holds that without skills-training this most complex of relationships will naturally work itself out successfully. But

Five levels of communication

5
Small talk, cliché conversation – 'Looks like rain again', 'How are you?'

4
Conversation on the facts and figures level – watch this, men especially!

3
Introducing personal ideas and opinions – beginning of real intimacy.

2
Sharing feelings and emotions – positive and negative feelings.

1
Mutual sharing, mutual empathy – peak communication, deep insight.

marriages today fall apart because contemporary marital expectations are different from those of the past.

Traditional marriages were held together because commitment took precedence over contentment. Even if you were not getting your needs fulfilled, you just hung in there. It's changed now. Today couples must possess necessary skills if their marriages are to be saved. Who does what, needs to be thoroughly explored before marriage. Family background will play a significant role in your attitude towards decision-making. When you have arguments, don't go, *grow*.

The story is told of a man and his wife. He would have a hard time at work; she would also have a hard time working at home. He used to come home and growl, and would make his wife feel bad. One day he said, 'Look, dear, I don't mean to hurt you but during the day the boss gets onto me so much I get into a bad mood, so listen. If I come home and my hat is turned around backwards, don't bother me for a while. Give me a few minutes with my newspaper. Then things will be all right.'

To ensure that a family unit thrives, not just survives, depends upon the 'Who does what' question being sorted out before marriage.

If conflict isn't handled properly it can become a destructive force allowing bitterness to dominate the relationship.

His wife thought about it, and said, 'You know, honey, I was thinking. Times get hard with me, too. So if you come home one day and you see my apron on the wrong way round, don't bother me.' Time went on and that was their agreement. One day the husband came home and his hat was turned around as he started up the path. His wife heard the car door slam, so she looked out of the window. The children had given her a hard time that day, so she turned her apron around. Before he could get to the door she threw it open. There he stood with his hat back to front, looking at her with her apron on the wrong way round. And do you know what they did? They laughed, just as you did!

Getting the gloves on
Is your marriage a duel or a duet? Do you just keep on fighting? While conflict is a normal part of most loving relationships, there are right and wrong ways of fighting. Alienating practices should be avoided. There's nothing wrong with the occasional argument. But even at these times there are rules to the game. Hitting below the belt is always out of order. A primary requirement is that couples develop the quality of active *listening*. How do you do that? Remember it this way:

MARS v VENUS

A book which has proved very popular is *Men are from Mars, Women are from Venus*. The author, John Gray, believes that understanding that men and women have different communication styles, emotional needs, and modes of behaviour, will resolve much of the conflict in marriages today. Some psychologists say these differences are because our brains are constructed differently, others say it is the result of how we are conditioned to act. Whatever the answer is, sometimes our partners act as if they come from a different planet.

MISTAKES MARTIANS AND VENUSIANS MAKE

Men, did you know?
John Gray states: 'Many times a woman just wants to share her feelings about her day, and her husband, thinking he's helping, interrupts her by offering a steady flow of solutions to her problems.' Men, listen, reflect back, empathize – don't solve.

Women, did you know?
Dr Gray states: 'To offer a man unsolicited advice is to presume that he doesn't know what to do or that he can't do it on his own.' That's why men are so upset when they are driving and their wife asks them if they are sure they know where they are going. Their response is, 'Of course I'm sure, and I'll prove it to you, even if it takes all night.'

The **L** of Listen stands for *look at me*. We're talking about eye contact here. Focus your full attention on your partner. Turn off the television and put down the paper. Mary Kay Ash, in her book *On People Management* says:
'I look directly at the person. Even if a gorilla were to walk into the room, I probably wouldn't notice it. I remember how offended I once was when I was having lunch with my sales manager, and every time a pretty waitress walked by, his eyes would follow her across the room. I felt insulted and kept thinking to myself, "That waitress's legs are more important to him that what I have to say. He's not listening to me. He doesn't care about me!" '

The **I** of Listen stands for *interest yourself*. Be interested in what you're about to hear. Block all other distractions from your mind. Don't presume you already know exactly what your partner is going to say. Don't mind-read and don't interrupt. Raise your eyebrows, nod your head, smile or laugh when appropriate. For a few minutes, nothing else in the world matters except hearing your partner out.

The **S** of Listen stands for *sit attentively*. We're talking body language now. Unfold your arms, rest your hands on your knees and lean forward in your chair. You are now displaying an open stance; one that makes it easier for your partner to talk to you; one that convinces your partner that you are really listening.

The **T** of Listen stands for *tell me you understand*. Sprinkle your attentive listening with appropriate phrases to show agreement, interest, and understanding. Your partner wants to know that you understand the ideas he or she is presenting. Try to think through what he or she is saying and fit it into your own experience. Resist the temptation to jump in with a solution – particularly you men! You can see the solution right in front of your face, but button your lips. She chose to talk to you rather than open an encyclopaedia because what she needs right now is not your knowledge but your presence. Just empathize.

The **E** of Listen stands for *encourage me*. Ask well-phrased questions. Give encouragement by asking questions that illustrate your interest. Don't probe; don't ask questions just to satisfy your craving for gossip. Don't simply use the exact words that you have heard; that does not demonstrate you can listen, it only shows that

> **What would you say is the best response to give to Mary who has just come home from work?**
>
> MARY
> 'Oh, my feet, they're so tired from standing all day.'
> BILL
> ❏ 'Hmm, sounds as if you need to wear more sensible shoes.'
> ❏ 'You need to know when to work and when to rest.'
> ❏ 'Sounds as if you've had an exhausting day.'
> ❏ 'My feet never ache like that.'
> ❏ 'You sound just like your mother.'
>
> I'll leave you and your spouse to sort that one out!

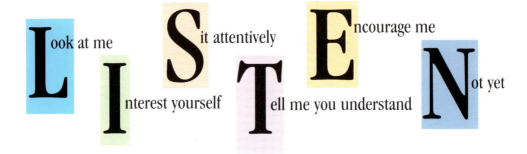

Look at me
Interest yourself
Sit attentively
Tell me you understand
Encourage me
Not yet

your ears are not blocked. Reflect back, using expressions such as, 'Are you saying you're upset because . . . '; 'I get the impression you are apprehensive about . . . '. If you are wrong your partner will correct you. Consider the case of Eric who comes home from work and says to Gail, 'I wish you would not talk on the phone in the evenings when I'm home.' Gail might respond, 'You feel irritated when I spend evenings on the phone talking to other people.

The **N** of Listen stands for *not yet*. Just when you're tempted to switch off, listen for thirty seconds longer.

A husband had really mastered the principles of active listening. When his wife started to talk to him, he put down his newspaper, turned to face her, and looked into her eyes. The wife was flustered. She said, 'Now you're deliberately listening just to confuse me.'

What you give is what you get
Recognize that the person you are in conflict with is your best friend. It is the person you have vowed to stay with for better or for worse.

Active listening is vital to effective communication – especially within marriage. Sooner, rather than later, both partners have to learn the art.

You two have now become one. 'Husbands,' the apostle Paul says, 'love your wives as your own bodies.' Don't think of her as separate from you. When you feel like taking a break – think about giving her a break. When you feel like putting your feet up – let her put her feet up. When you make yourself a drink – make her one too. And you'll be the better for it. God has designed marriage in a particular fashion. It is impossible for one partner to suffer and the other to prosper.

God has arranged marriage in a unique way. It is impossible for one partner to be down and the other

Selfishness is the key to marital breakdown. Selflessness is the key to marital success. When you feel like taking a break – think about giving her a break.

up. Whatever she does will affect you. And whatever you do will affect her. So if you refuse and abuse her – you will feel it yourself. Slap her and you're only slapping yourself. Bad-mouth her and you're only hurting your own body. Why? Because you're not two any more, you're one. Your emotional well-being is closely related to your spouse's well-being. It is now impossible for your spouse to be sad and you to be happy. Therefore, don't try to defeat your spouse, because if she is defeated, you are defeated. It is to your own advantage to have what we call win-win situations whenever there is conflict! That's why the Bible says, 'For since a man and his wife are now one, a man is really doing himself a favour and loving himself when he loves his wife.' (Ephesians 5:28, LB.) No wonder H. Page Williams entitled his book – written to men only – *Do Yourself a Favour: Love Your Wife!*

Because we live in close proximity to our spouses, conflict is bound to occur. While the Bible states, 'It is not good that the man should be alone' (Genesis 2:18, KJV), yet sometimes conflict is nothing more than a cry for space. Children, money, sex, stress, in-laws – you name it. I want to suggest eight easy-to-remember rules of conflict-solving:

Your emotional well-being is closely related to that of your spouse. If she is defeated, so are you. When there is conflict a 'win-win' situation must be created; never 'win-lose'.

Sorting it all out
C stands for *choose the best time and place*. Generally, the sooner the better. The Bible says, 'Don't let the sun go down on your anger.' Don't let it drag on, but don't try to squeeze it in just before you go

to sleep! No, not at night. And not at mealtimes. Too many fights escalate unnecessarily because one partner opens fire when it is wholly inconvenient for the spouse. Try to select the time and place *together*. Businesses and church committees can schedule times for handling disputes, why not marriage? You will discover that most conflicts really can be postponed until there is adequate time to deal with them. Do not, however, postpone them indefinitely.

A discussion you've never had in *your* home!

HE: 'I need more socks.'
SHE: 'So go and buy some.'
HE: 'I thought you could pick them up since you'll be out this afternoon anyway.'
SHE: 'You're just like your father – always ordering somebody around.'
HE: 'Oh, yeah? At least my mother could cook!'
SHE: 'Well, she's a mess herself! She hasn't had a decent haircut in years.'
HE: 'You ought to do something with *your* hair. It's ridiculous.'
SHE: 'Not that there's room in the bathroom with your stuff scattered everywhere . . . .'

O stands for *one problem at a time*. The more problems you bring up at one time, the less likelihood of solving any of them. So stay on just one problem until you solve it. Avoid dragging up old scores and arguments. Don't be hysterical or historical. Some people ought to be archaeologists, they just love digging up the past. Old wounds get opened and the issues get confused. Agree that if it's more than six months old, then it's *inadmissible evidence!*

N stands for *no-nos to remember*. Here are some no-nos. No name-calling. No wild threats of divorce or suicide or withholding of sexual intimacy. No remarks about in-laws or relatives. No put-downs about appearance or intelligence. No yelling. No interruptions. No emotional outbursts. No sarcasm. No silent treatment. No mixed messages; you know, making sure your partner knows you are angry, but denying it at the same time. Joan asks, 'What's wrong, darling? Is it something I said, something I did, something I forgot to do?' Clive retorts, 'Oh, it's nothing,' and then proceeds to fold his arms, button his mouth, heave a sigh and look hurt. If something's wrong, say so! And remember, no violence. There's a list for you to remember!

F stands for *find all possible solutions*. Brainstorm every possible solution. Doesn't matter how far-fetched they seem. Just make a list of them. Don't fuel an argument by using expressions such as 'you always' or 'you never'. Be open. Remember, the goal is not to see who is at fault or who should get the blame, rather, your purpose is to find a solution.

L stands for *list the most likely solutions*. Make an intelligent choice now. Evaluate each solution. Share together how you feel about the consequences of each solution. Use I-statements which focus on personal feeling, rather than you-statements which can sound accusing.

I stands for *implement the decision*. Decide who will do what, where, and when. Remember, only friendly negotiation really solves the problem. If you win an argument and she doesn't speak to you for a week, what have you really won? Don't win an argument and lose a friend.

COMMON CAUSES OF CONFLICT IN MARRIAGE

* 'His job is everything.'
* 'Too much month left at the end of the money.'
* 'I always dreaded having a mother-in-law.'
* 'We disagreed about our daughter.'
* 'He would never talk about his feelings.'
* 'The criticism just wore me out.'
* 'Mid-life crisis.'
* 'He thinks sex starts in the bedroom.'
* 'The house is a mess' or 'The house is too clean.'
* 'I didn't expect this . . . .'

C stands for *choose the most acceptable solution*. That is, the solution closest to satisfying both of you; and commit yourself to it. Some compromising may be necessary; some give and take. Be prepared to negotiate and modify. You'll have to negotiate, you may even have to compromise, but there'll be no winner. It took two to make a conflict and it'll take two to resolve it. And finally:

T stands for *tell it in love*. Say it straight, but say it right. The Bible says, 'Speak the truth in love.' State your feelings openly and respectfully. Keep your voice down. As much as you can, stay calm. You can learn to stay reasonable. *Choose not to argue.*

Starting all over again

The devil delights in getting us to think that our situation is too far gone to be saved. He boasted when he got Abraham to fall. He boasted when he got David to fall. He boasted when he got Solomon to fall. But the good news is that the same Solomon repented and asked God to strengthen him one more time. And he wrote in Proverbs 24:16: 'A just man falls seven times, and rises up again.'

Not only Solomon, but David fell on his face in repentance and cried out: 'Create in me a new, clean heart, O God, filled with clean thoughts and right desires.' (Psalm 51:10, LB.) We serve a God who is the God of a second chance. You say, 'But I've reached rock-bottom.' Well, we serve a God who made the rocks! The only real mistake is the mistake from which we learn nothing. Corrie ten Boom, author of *The Hiding Place*, said:

'Once I visited a weavers' school, where the students were making beautiful patterns. I asked, "When you make a mistake, must you cut it out and start from the beginning?" A student said, "No. Our teacher is such a great artist that when we make a mistake, he uses it to improve the beauty of the pattern."'

God delights in using our mistakes for His glory. Somebody said life is like an onion. You peel it a layer at a time – and sometimes you weep. Ah, but you and your spouse can start again! And if you will only come to Him, you will Hear him say to you as He said to the woman caught in the act of adultery: 'Neither do I condemn you. Go and sin no more.'

I don't know what your situation is today. But I do know that there is forgiveness with God. God looks upon you as if you have never sinned. Because of the death of Jesus, you can start again.

LOVEWORK ON CHAPTER 5

10 and 10 DIALOGUE

1 Choose a topic together. Each spouse will write a letter to the other for ten minutes on that topic, without conferring (even if it means going into another room).

2 Let your letter be on a pleasant topic; whatever the topic, begin your letter with a term of endearment ('Hi, Sweetheart' as opposed to 'Hey, woman', for example).

3 Whatever the topic, let your first paragraph contain an element of praise for something positive you saw your spouse do or be.

4 Use any feeling words that you can. Be personal, how did *you* feel about it?

5 Don't worry if you're not much of a writer. This is not an English composition assignment, but you will see that sometimes the pen is mightier than the mouth and there is a tremendous richness inside us that is just waiting to be expressed.

6 After writing for ten minutes, exchange letters and come close together, knee to knee.

7 Read and discuss the letters for the final ten minutes. Read your spouse's letter to yourself *twice,* once for the head and once for the heart. This exercise allows a quiet spouse equal time with a dominant partner. In reading the letter a dominant partner will not be able to interrupt his or her spouse as he or she would in purely oral discourse.

8 Discuss both letters, how they made you feel. Some letters will take much courage to express; some people will try to pour so much love into them. Be sensitive as you dialogue.

9 Keep the letters if you so desire. Some, because of the content, have burned their letters together, cried together, and made a new start together. Treasure them or trash them.

10 Schedule another 10 and 10; you will never find time, so why not *make time now?*

DIALOGUE TOPICS

* Our communicating would improve if I would . . .
* The beauty I see in you is the following . . .
* When we have passed away I would like others to say of our marriage . . .
* The characteristics I appreciated in you today were . . .
* I was thankful today for . . .
* Something new I discovered about myself is . . .
* I find it difficult to communicate with others because . . .
* A holiday that would be fun for us could be . . .
* If we could build a dream house, it would . . .
* Some of my teen frustrations were . . .
* I feel weak when . . .
* I have feelings of pure pleasure when . . .
* I wish I could stop . . .
* A step I'm taking to improve my character is . . .
* When you express your love to me I feel . . .
* What have been two of the happiest times that I have shared with you?
* What are the qualities that I like best about me? How does this make me feel?
* What are the qualities that I like best about you? How does this make me feel?
* What are the qualities that I like best about us? How does this make me feel?
* How could I be more open with you? How does this make me feel?
* How could I help you to be more open with me? How does this make me feel?
* The ways I show my love for you in our relationship are . . .

6 Marital sex, God's wedding gift

'It is a good principle for a man to have no physical contact with women. Nevertheless, because casual liaisons are so prevalent, let every man have his own wife and every woman her own husband. The husband should give his wife what is due to her as his wife, and the wife should be as fair to her husband. The wife has no longer full rights over her own person, but shares them with her husband. In the same way the husband shares his personal rights with his wife. Do not cheat each other of normal sexual intercourse, unless of course you both decide to abstain temporarily to make special opportunity for fasting and prayer. But afterwards you should resume relations as before, or you will expose yourselves to the obvious temptation of the Devil.'

(1 CORINTHIANS 7:1-5, JBP.)

Sex is a gift of God. Sex is, in fact, God's wedding gift to every married couple and it is a gift He does not want opened early. Sexual intercourse is a means of communication at the deepest level. Sexual satisfaction, as with other communication in marriage, is a gradual achievement, a process in which the married couple in a committed relationship will learn and grow together through sexual ecstasy and frustration. True sexual fulfilment comes as a result of loving expression with one's spouse, and the manner of that expression is not dictated.

Take time

Sex is a celebration of love. As the years move on, sex can often end up as what you do when you've done everything else. The physical excitement may have gone out of the relationship. Couples need to be reminded that in the earlier stages of the relationship, quality time was invested in the whole sexual process to ensure mutual pleasure.

For a woman to enjoy the act of sex she needs to feel wanted and loved. To bury your head in the newspaper, watch the television until night, and then announce to your wife, 'It's time', is a recipe for failure. Foreplay is not something which begins in the bedroom. While a woman may take twenty minutes or more to be fully aroused for sex, it must be recognized that sex begins when you help her in the kitchen and touch her lovingly and tenderly. Somebody said it this way, 'Men, if you want to be in heaven at eleven you'd better start before seven!'

There is a four-stage process used to describe sexual response:
1 the arousal stage
2 the excitement stage
3 the climax stage
4 the resolution stage

We will look at each of these stages individually.

SEXUAL RESPONSE
❑ **Arousal stage.** A person may become sexually stimulated by various sensory inputs. Men are generally considered to be visually stimulated; they may be aroused simply by looking at a woman. Sexual arousal for a man begins with the erection of the penis, which takes place when columns in the penis containing spongy, erective tissue get filled with blood (known as *vasocongestion*). The veins in the penis constrict, thereby trapping the blood in the columns and causing the penis to become erect.

Arousal also comes from a kiss, the tone of a voice, the smell of a perfume. The most direct stimulation, however, is touch. There are areas of the body which produce a sexual response when touched; these are called *erogenous zones*. During the arousal stage the woman's breasts may enlarge and the nipples become erect and increase slightly in diameter. It is the *clitoris*, however, which is known as the trigger for female sexual arousal. Located about one inch above the entrance to the vagina, the tip of the clitoris contains a high concentration of touch-sensitive nerves.

During this arousal stage a woman's *labia majora* (Latin for 'major lips'), which join over the vaginal opening, pull back from the vaginal opening and flatten. Sustained tenderness and sensitivity should be exercised by the man as he gently massages the hood over the clitoris for his wife's enjoyment. The clitoris is not physiologically necessary for intercourse to take place, but many believe God has designed it simply for the woman's pleasure. For the Christian, the joy of sex is found not just in the receiving of pleasure, but also in the giving.

❏ **Excitement stage.** The arousal stage merges into the excitement stage, which is a more highly aroused state of sexual stimulation. The glans, located at the head of the penis, is the most sensitive part of a man's sexual anatomy when touched. In the excitement stage, penile erection reaches its maximum and seminal fluid starts to flow. The vagina expands to become a receptacle for the seminal fluid. With increased foreplay and the stimulation of the erogenous zones, at the invitation of the woman, the penis is inserted into the vagina and genital stimulation continues as the couple move rhythmically. Both heart rate and breathing become more rapid as the level of excitement increases. Vasocongestion increases and sexual sensitivity is heightened.

❏ **Climax stage.** The climax stage is characterized by a series of contractions of the pelvic muscles which are accompanied by pleasurable sensations of release, usually lasting up to fifteen seconds. For two or three seconds, men experi-

ence a sensation when they know ejaculation is about to take place. It is the semen flowing out by contractions of muscles at the base of the penis which produces the pleasure of orgasm. For the man, these contractions occur less than a second apart. For the woman, her contractions may last up to thirty seconds. The majority of women require clitoral stimulation for orgasm to take place.

❑ **Resolution stage.** The resolution stage follows the climax stage and manifests itself differently in men and women. Men enter what is known as a *refractory period* when they are incapable of restimulation. Some women may be capable of further immediate arousal and multiple orgasms and, at least, desire the husband to be affectionate rather than simply turn over and go to sleep. This stage has also been called the *afterglow*, where body functions return to normal levels and husband and wife embrace.

SEXUAL DYSFUNCTIONS

In many cases problems occur in the giving or receiving of sexual satisfaction. While physical causes are by no means rare, the majority of sexual problems have psychological causes. There are three major sexual dysfunctions in males which require treatment by a qualified psychosexual therapist:

❑ **Impotence**. Firstly, there is impotence or erectile malfunction. A primary dysfunction is said to occur when the male has never had an erection; such cases require sustained attention from a sex therapist.

A secondary dysfunction is said to occur when penetration has been possible at some time. Such impotence can be overcome. There

Alcohol is a major cause of impotence.

may be various reasons for the occurrence of impotence at this time. There may have been a traumatic first experience of sex. This may have involved religious taboos, fear of impregnating one's partner, fear of sexually-transmitted disease, or fear of contracting or imparting AIDS. Secondary impotence can also be caused by alcohol, tiredness (particularly in the case of shift work), and prescribed, as well as recreational, drugs.

Impotence is also age related. It is estimated that 50 per cent of men at the age of 70 have frequent erectile failures. The good news is that the other 50 per cent do not!

❑ **Premature ejaculation.** Secondly, there is premature ejaculation. This is ejaculation before penetration or immediately after (that is up to two minutes, or not maintaining an erection long enough for a partner to reach a climax 50 per cent of the time). Causes of premature ejaculation include:

high expectations of the male's performance;

intercourse when accompanied by the fear of discovery;

collusion by a woman who has gone off sex and wants the experience over quickly.

The prognosis is good for such dysfunctions.

❑ **Retarded ejaculation.** Thirdly, there is retarded ejaculation. This is very rare, but it is the inability to ejaculate in intercourse. There may be medical reasons for this, or psychological causes, such as the fear of getting the woman pregnant, fear of damaging the woman, fear of castration, lack of commitment, the presence of power struggles in a relationship, and even one's religious background. The prognosis for such cases is good; therapists are able to achieve significant results.

There are three major sexual dysfunctions in females which require treatment by a qualified psychosexual therapist:

❑ **Vaginal tightening.** Firstly, there is vaginismus. This is the involuntary contraction of muscles around the vagina at the possibility of penetration. It involves a tightening of the muscles as if one is trying to stop urinating. Some women may suffer from what is known as penile phobia as a result of a trauma connected with the vagina such as incest, rape, medical trauma, or even events at the start of menstruation. Psychosexual therapists will often recommend the Keagle exercises for vaginismus. These involve pelvic exercises done on the floor. The prognosis is good for such cases.

❑ **Pain on intercourse.** Secondly, there is dyspareunia, which is pain on intercourse. This female condition is usually due to a lack of arousal coupled with inadequate lubrication. It may be linked to a medical factor, but if not there may be a fear of intimacy, or it may be linked to past traumas such as a traumatic childbirth experience. The prognosis for such cases is also good.

❏ **Orgasmic failure.** Thirdly, there is orgasmic dysfunction. While it is estimated that 75 per cent of women require clitoral stimulation for an orgasm, 50 per cent of women are never orgasmic in intercourse. This may be as a result of bad childhood messages, an over-protected background, power struggles within the relationship, or unresolved conflicts with one's father. Psychosexual therapists will often treat such cases with a nine-step programme.

Sexual fulfilment is the work of years, and God has designed that it take place within the loving security of marriage. Lewis Smedes says in his book *Sex for Christians:* 'The marriage of committed love is God's design for sexual freedom .... Here, in this settled union, two people can adventure into sexual growth, work through sexual pain and frustration, love through the rise and fall of erotic desire.'

It is a gift from God, not to be abused or misused, not to be bargained with, not to be shared outside of the relationship. God has placed a sacred circle around the sexual experience of a husband and wife. No children, no siblings, no in-laws, no friends must invade this private sphere.

AIDS

AIDS is a disease of global proportions. It first became apparent in the US in the early eighties when doctors began noticing a rare skin cancer (Kaposi's sarcoma) occurring more frequently in homosexual male patients. As early as 1986 it was estimated that worldwide there were between five and ten million people infected with HIV. In 1998 the estimated figure was 30 to 40 million.

HIV is a virus which attacks people regardless of their age, sex, colour of skin or sexual orientation. It is also no respecter of religious beliefs. It is a consequence of sin, one of the many we face in this life.

Many people who have caught AIDS would not regard themselves as promiscuous. Sometimes you hear a person say, 'It's not fair! How could I have AIDS? I've only had sex with one person!' Until recently it was reckoned that men and women, on average, had sex with six different people in their lifetime. And those six partners with thirty-six more .... So one person could receive sexually-transmitted diseases (STDs) from up to 40,000 other people! It only needs *one* person to pass on an infection.

Immune system
AIDS is a viral disease that destroys the immune system, hence the name, Acquired Immune Deficiency Syndrome. With a lowered resistance to disease, a person becomes vulnerable to infections otherwise non-fatal, and the immediate cause of death is often a rare form of pneumonia or cancer. Every fifteen seconds, someone is infected with HIV (the Human Immunodeficiency Virus), the virus causing AIDS. HIV is found in the fluids exchanged during sexual intercourse (men's semen and women's vaginal fluids). HIV is spreading at an increasing rate in almost every country. No community or country can claim that it has been able to stop this spread.

There is no vaccine or cure for AIDS. One in 250 of the world's adult population is already infected. There are between thirty and forty million people infected with HIV globally. There will be ten million AIDS orphans in Africa alone. In many African countries, 50 per cent of hospital beds are occupied by AIDS patients. The fastest spread of HIV is in Asia, particularly India and Thailand.

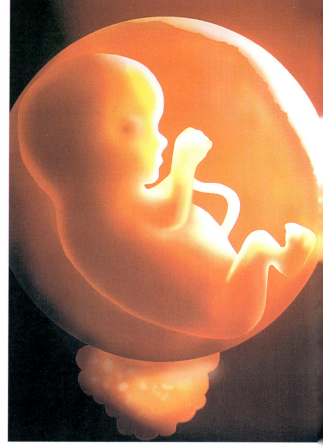
HIV can be passed on from an infected mother to her baby before, during or after birth.

Sexually-transmitted diseases and the number of sexual partners increase the risk of HIV infection. Sexual intercourse, whether heterosexual or homosexual, is a major way for HIV to be passed from one person to another. This is how most people in the world with HIV become infected. HIV can be passed on from an infected mother to her baby before, during or after birth. Babies born to infected mothers carry antibodies from the mother in their blood. These may take about a year to disappear. Only then is it possible to test accurately if the baby is HIV positive. There is also a small risk of infection from the breast milk of an infected mother.

What does HIV do?
The Human Immunodeficiency Virus (HIV) has a protein coat which binds mostly to one kind of white blood cell called the T helper cell or CD4 cell. The CD4 cells are an essential part of our body's defences against disease. Once attached to the cell, the virus injects genes to programme the cell to make up thousands of new HIV particles. Eventually the host cell dies and releases all the new viruses into the blood. The infected CD4 cell will now pass on HIV into other healthy cells of the body.

As the viruses invade more and more CD4 cells, they can no longer help defend the body against illness. Eventually the body's defences become so weakened that the illnesses and infections we call AIDS can develop. We say someone has AIDS when the virus has

An AIDS researcher analyses samples of human blood. HIV attacks white blood cells causing a steady decline in the immune system, eventually leading to AIDS.

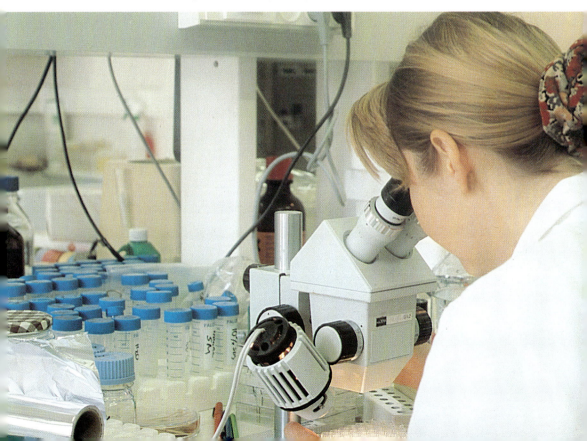

WHAT IS SAFE SEX?

SAFE
Close relationships that stop short of sexual intercourse.
Staying a virgin till marriage and marrying an uninfected partner.
Staying faithful to one partner for life, neither partner ever injecting drugs.

LOWER RISK
Sex outside of marriage using a condom or non-penetrative sex. Do not place an inordinate amount of faith in the condom. As a birth control device they have a failure rate of between 10 and 30 per cent. Why should we trust them to protect us any better from AIDS or other STDs?

HIGHER RISK
Sex outside of marriage without a condom.
(How can you be sure of your partner?)

VERY HIGH RISK
Sex without a condom with an infected partner or partners.

weakened the body so much that certain new illnesses are developing. As a result, organisms such as fungi, viruses, and parasites that can live inside most people without causing disease can cause serious infections in people with HIV. When these infections occur, or when the number of CD4 cells drops below a certain level, a person with HIV infection is said to have AIDS.

If the 'helper' cells are weakened, the chest can be infected. It gets harder to breathe – and you may die. Your gut can get infected, so you can't absorb the goodness in your food. You lose weight, you feel very weak, and often have diarrhoea. Cancers may grow, causing problems on the skin or inside the body. Another virus can destroy your eyesight and infections attacking your brain can make it hard to remember things. People with AIDS are often unwell for long periods between times of illness. Fifty per cent of the people infected with HIV will become ill within ten years, many of the rest after fifteen years. Once infected, it is almost certain you will sooner or later develop AIDS.

You cannot tell by outward appearance who has HIV. You can be tested for infection at a special hospital clinic. The test looks to see if there are any HIV antibodies in the bloodstream. Antibodies develop as part of the body's natural defence system against viruses and germs. The antibodies against HIV can take around three months to develop. It is important to wait

AIDS

You are famous!
Those who have not seen you do not
  believe you.
Those who have not heard about you do
  not understand you.
You bring destruction to the rich and to
  the poor,
Also to the great and small.
You leave no traces.

You are a warlord!
Whenever you are around,
You fully engage yourself.
Those who cannot break you must join you.
Those who want to fight you challenge them,
You completely destroy them.
They lose sight of everything.

You are a thief!
You steal joy and happiness,
Confidence and pride.
You grow inside like a love herb.
You wait stealthily to strike.
The one you have captured, you do not
  have to ask
Because he is always in bed.
He fights and resists but you eventually
  destroy him.

You are fearful!
Wherever you are there is weeping.
Wherever you have struck there is death.
Wherever you are going there is confusion.
Where you are not known you do as
  you please.
Whenever we talk about you, we whisper.
Whenever we think about you, we see a grave.
You are fearful!

Mothers! Gird up your loins!
Arm yourselves and charge!
Be courageous and tell them, while they
  can still listen.
Explain to them the pain, the dangers
  and hurt.
When you do not know what to say,
Go out and seek knowledge.
Mothers, this is a challenge!

I am not putting fear into you.
This is an assurance you will die.
When you allow your feelings
To control your mind
Then you deceive your conscience
And pretend as if it is not there.
It will kill you!

AFRICAN POET, in *ON COMMON GROUND*, edited by Zandile Nhlengetwa, et al.

TOM'S STORY

Tom is a lorry driver. He's infected with the virus causing AIDS, but doesn't know. Tom has in turn passed the virus on to Mary and Sam; he is bisexual. Still not knowing he's infected, Tom marries Janet. A year later, she's infected too. One day Tom is rushed to hospital with an unusual type of pneumonia. Now the doctor tells him he has AIDS. Through Tom's infected partner, six people become ill, some of whom Tom has never even met . . . . Tom could have been infected in one of at least three different ways. What are they?

ANSWER
- *He could be infected by sexual intercourse with an infected man, woman, boy or girl.*
- *He could be infected by injecting drugs using a shared needle and syringe.*
- *He might have been given infected blood or blood products. (Prior to 1985, for example, supplies of blood in the UK were not screened for HIV.)*

at least twelve weeks after possible infection to have the test in order to have accurate results. Deciding to have the test is a traumatic period of time. Counselling should always be offered before taking the test, and will certainly be needed after receiving the result.

From a toilet seat?
HIV is a virus which does not survive easily outside the body. It is not spread through food or water, by sharing cups or glasses, or by coughing and sneezing. There is no danger of becoming infected through everyday social contact. There is no need to worry about becoming infected with HIV by touch or sharing objects used by an infected person, such as cups, cutlery, glasses, food, clothes, towels, toilet seats, door knobs, or swimming pools. HIV cannot be transmitted through such things as mosquito bites, hugging, or giving blood where sterile equipment and disposable needles are used, or receiving tested blood.

Christian response
People with HIV and AIDS, and those who care for them, may face loneliness, isolation, prejudice and

lack of understanding for a variety of reasons. In many places there are support groups to offer friendship and counsel. Victims of AIDS, like leprosy sufferers in Bible times, carry a stigma in society; and like the man who was born blind, referred to in John's gospel, chapter 9, so often we want to know, 'Who sinned, this man or . . . .' We want to know the details of the story, often for purposes of gossip rather than ministry. As Christians, our calling is not to isolate but to minister. Jesus said, 'Inasmuch as you have done it unto the least of these my children, you have done it unto me.'

Protect children against a deadly inheritance.

LOVEWORK ON CHAPTER 6

Sexual understanding within marriage

Complete the following questionnaire independently, then discuss together.

1 It is important that sexual intercourse results in orgasm for me:
❏ usually
❏ sometimes
❏ rarely

2 I prefer sexual intercourse approximately ☐ times a week.

3 The most enjoyable position for intercourse for me is:
❏ man above
❏ woman above
❏ rear entry
❏ side (face to face)
❏ other (specify)

4 Before intercourse, foreplay is:
❏ very important for me
❏ somewhat important for me
❏ rarely important for me
❏ very important for my spouse

❏ somewhat important for my spouse
❏ rarely important for my spouse

5 When it comes to ambience, the following things help put me in the mood for love:
❏ music (type)
_____

❏ lighting (type)
_____

❏ clothing (type)
_____

❏ food/drink (type)
_____

❏ touching (type)
_____

❏ words/deeds (type)
_____

6 I prefer to have sexual intercourse in our bedroom:
❏ exclusively
❏ sometimes in other places

7 Contraception is the responsibility of:
❏ wife
❏ husband
❏ husband and wife

8 My attitude towards and knowledge about sex have come from:
❏ media
❏ peers
❏ readings
❏ relative (specify)
_____

9 In our sexual relationship I want my spouse to be the initiator:
❏ always
❏ sometimes
❏ rarely
❏ never

10 During sexual intercourse I prefer:
❏ my spouse to know intuitively what I like
❏ communicating to my spouse what I like and where I like to be touched
❏ letting passion take its course

11 My greatest deficiency in the area of sex is:
❏ knowledge of sexual anatomy
❏ knowledge of sexual technique
❏ inability to verbalize my desires or unhappiness
❏ other (specify)
_____

12 Rank the following as to the purpose of sex:
❏ procreation (childbirth)
❏ necessary duty of marriage
❏ relief of tension
❏ mutual expression of love, designed by God

7 Children, the gift of marriage

'Children, the right thing for you to do is to obey your parents as those whom God has set over you. The first commandment to contain a promise was: Honour thy father and thy mother that it may be well with thee, and that thou mayest live long on the earth. Fathers, don't over-correct your children or make it difficult for them to obey the commandment. Bring them up with Christian teaching and discipline.'

(EPHESIANS 6:1-4, JBP.)

Dr Leslie Pollard tells the story of how, as a single pastor, he was blessed by a loving congregation. They were so happy with the way things were – for a while. 'Oh, Pastor,' they exclaimed, 'it's wonderful to have you with us and your ministry, but you do not have a wife. Wouldn't it be a marvellous thing if there was a Mrs Pollard!' In time, God blessed Dr Pollard with a lovely wife. The church rejoiced. Leslie and Prudence had an inspired ministry together and the church was very happy – for a while. 'Oh, Pastor,' they declared, 'it's wonderful to have you and your wife in team ministry, but you do not have any children. Wouldn't it be a marvellous thing if there was a child in your family!' In time, God blessed the Drs Pollard with a lovely baby girl. The church rejoiced.

The Pollard family was happy and the church was very happy – for a while. 'Oh, Pastor,' they declared, 'it's wonderful to have you and your wife and your daughter, but only one child, Pastor! The child will be lonely. Wouldn't it be a marvellous thing if there was another child in your family!' In time, God blessed the Drs Pollard with another beautiful daughter. The church rejoiced. The Pollard family was so happy and the church was very happy – for a while. 'Oh, Pastor,' they declared, 'it's wonderful that we have you and your wife and your children, but both girls, Pastor! Wouldn't it be a marvellous thing if there was a boy!' Dr Pollard says, 'I looked squarely at them and said as firmly as I could, "The shop is closed." ' Whether single or married, childfree or quiver full, you are whole and complete in Jesus Christ.

Discipline

I often think the reason why some people want young couples to hurry up and have children is because they can't stand the freedom and joy the young couple are experiencing.... They are struggling with their four children and they want this carefree couple to join them in their misery! That's why in some parts of America they changed the term from child*less* to child*free*. Children and discipline – a real issue, isn't it?

A parent once asked at one of our seminars, 'What do you do if your child is consistently lying?' With all questions such as this there is a *preventative* answer and a *redemptive* answer. •On the redemptive side, discipline will need to be applied which will enforce acceptable and unacceptable boundaries that are going to be tolerated by you. Perpetual prevarication or lying will require psychological help. •From a preventative perspective, parents, you have nine years to bond your child to yourself. After that, your child will be more influenced by what he or she sees (for example, on television), hears (for example, from teachers and peers), and reads, than by what you say.

So strive to become your children's best friend. Help them to feel comfortable sharing confidences with you. Parents, be vigilant, walk with your eyes open. In fact, you must actually be the eyes and ears for your children. It will require courage because your children may often misinterpret your good intentions, but you must recognize more than they do the power of peer relations. When parents are unaware of the whereabouts of their children, there is a greater susceptibility to risk-taking behaviour.

Adolescents are far more susceptible because of peer pressure to enter into risk-taking behaviour during the unsupervised hours between 3 and 6pm than any other time during the day. In the US, twenty-two million children, between 50 and 95 per cent of all school-aged children, are left unsupervised between 3 and 6pm. Many of the unsupervised children spend this time with their peers. Most adolescent girls who become pregnant do so between the hours of 3 and 6pm *in their own home.* Ellen White wrote, in *Counsels to Parents, Teachers and Students,* page 120:

'Parents should remember that association with those of lax morals and coarseness of character will have a detrimental influence upon the youth. If they fail to choose proper society for their children, if they allow them to associate with

youth of questionable morals, they place them, or permit them to place themselves, in a school where lessons of depravity are taught and practised. . . . Parents, guard the principles and habits of your children as the apple of the eye. Allow them to associate with no one with whose character you are not well acquainted. Permit them to form no intimacy until you are assured that it will do them no harm. Accustom your children to trust your judgement and experience.'

Contraception and abortion
If you are struggling to supervise the one child you already have, prayerfully consider whether God will want you to have another. Although the RSPCA urges otherwise, you *can* give a dog back after Christmas – not so your child. Human sexuality has two functions: one as an expression of love, the other to propagate the race. While the Bible says to us, ' "Be fruitful and multiply," ' the same verse in Genesis 1:28 says, ' "Fill the earth *and subdue it.*" ' (RAV, emphasis ours). This Scripture requires us to be responsible for our environment and includes practising responsible birth control.

As Christians we not only permit but also promote the use of contraceptives, particularly to minimize the human suffering arising from over-population. Believers participate in most forms of contraception. Some prefer natural methods, for example, the rhythm method. Others prefer hormonal methods, such as the pill. Others, mechanical methods, for example the coil. Abortion, however, is not an

From the earliest stages of childhood, children need to learn that they can trust the judgement and experience of their parents.

A CHILD'S TEN COMMANDMENTS TO PARENTS

1 My hands are small; please don't expect perfection whenever I make a bed, draw a picture, or throw a ball. My legs are short; please slow down so that I can keep up with you.

2 My eyes have not seen the world as yours have; please let me explore safely: don't restrict me unnecessarily.

3 Housework will always be there. I'm only little for such a short time – please take time to explain things to me about this wonderful world, and do so willingly.

4 My feelings are tender; please be sensitive to my needs; don't nag me all day long. (You wouldn't want to be nagged for your inquisitiveness.) Treat me as you would like to be treated.

5 I am a special gift from God; please treasure me as God intended you to do, holding me accountable for my actions, giving me guidelines to live by, and disciplining me in a loving manner.

6 I need your encouragement and your praise to grow. Please go easy on the criticism; remember you can criticize **the things I do** without criticizing me.

7 Please give me the freedom to make decisions concerning myself. Permit me to fail, so that I can learn from my mistakes. Then someday I'll be prepared to make the kinds of decisions life requires of me.

8 Please don't redo things for me after I've done them. Somehow that makes me feel that my efforts didn't quite measure up to your expectations. I know it's hard, but please don't try to compare me with my brother.

9 Please don't be afraid to go away for a weekend, leaving us with a responsible person whom you trust. Kids need space from parents, just as parents need space from kids. Besides, it's a great way to show us kids that your marriage is very special.

10 Please take me to church regularly, setting a good example for me to follow. I enjoy learning more about God.

Adapted from *PARENTHOOD WITHOUT HASSLES (WELL, ALMOST)* by Dr Kevin Leman.

acceptable form of birth control.

Sexual intercourse should be participated in within the confines of a committed marital relationship. Where this has not been the case and pregnancy has resulted, studies show that it is more common for whites to participate in abortion than for blacks. Sociologist Stephen Grunlan states in his book, *Marriage and the Family: A Christian Perspective:* 'White teenagers are seven times as likely as black teenagers to terminate a pregnancy by abortion, whereas black teenagers are twice as likely as white teenagers to keep their illegitimate child.'

Where an unplanned and unwanted pregnancy does occur, adoptions should be chosen over abortion. Most abortions are simply acts of child abuse carried out prematurely.

Abuse

Some time ago I received the following letter. The loneliness and isolation of the person – sexually abused within the family – is acute to the point of being unbearable. It has an effect on every aspect of the person's life. I quote a portion of the letter:

'Dear Dr Brown,

'The painful experiences of my childhood were quite a long time ago as I am now 32. It's an enormous weight for me that I should still be struggling over experiences that I felt were behind me, but my family (husband and two children) went through some experiences recently and a huge wound was torn open. The pain and filth has so overwhelmed me that I am not coping with normal, ordinary life. I try so very hard to, but I can't, so I wrote to you early one morning. One night some

A young person who is sexually abused within the family experiences an almost unbearable sense of loneliness and isolation.

three years ago I needed to talk, so I sat and wrote. I enclose what I wrote that night, for I could still write it now:

' "I feel such sadness and loneliness. I am so full of pain, is there no one to share it with?

' "Oh, who can I talk to? Where are my friends? Did I ever have any? Where do you get the confidence to seek help? Who will give me the time? Who will not destroy me as I expose my weakness? I cannot find anyone! Where do I go? What can I do? I want to run and find a place of rest, a hole that's soft and safe. But life doesn't permit. Who will care for my loved ones while I am gone? Will I ever return? What damage would it do to them? It's a burden too great to bear. There's too much at risk for me to rest awhile.

' "Who will come and help? Who will come and care? Who sees my pain? Do I hide it so well that no one can tell? Or is this life? Pain, weakness, overweighed with pressure, stress, debt, repetitious exhaustion?

' "I have no way of knowing for this is all I've known.

' " 'Have you not heard? The Lord is . . . the Creator of the ends of the earth. He will *not* grow *tired* or *weary* and His understanding no one can fathom.' "

'Perhaps I should go to a counsellor, but does talking about the pain help soothe it or magnify it? Many thanks for your time and encouragement.'

It's worth taking time to respond (see, for example, pages 112, 113). It's also worth taking time just to weep. Adults, our job is to protect our children. The Bible's medical writer states, ' "Woe to the man who does the tempting. If he were thrown into the sea with a huge rock tied to his neck, he would be far better off than facing the punishment in store for those who harm these little children. I am warning you." ' (Luke 17:1-3, LB.) Life is hard for our children without us burdening them any more. That's why Scripture declares, 'Fathers, do not provoke your children to anger; but bring them up in the discipline and instruction of the Lord.' (Ephesians 6:4, NASB.)

MAJOR ISSUES CONFRONTING YOUNG PEOPLE TODAY

❑ lack of self worth ❑ family difficulties ❑ depressions ❑ clarifying values ❑ accepting their physical appearance ❑ interpersonal relations ❑ moral weakness ❑ guilt ❑ loneliness ❑ career choice ❑ fear ❑ religion

The teenage years are a time of intense bewilderment, confusion, searching, testing, and rebelling. Unfortunately, we are called to make some of our most important decisions at adolescence, the least rational period of our lives, when we don't want to listen to the

IN THE EVENT OF RAPE

'I need to ask you about something which happened to me a few months ago. I was raped on the way home from work one night. I have not talked to anyone about it except my doctor – no, I wasn't pregnant but a worse problem still haunts me. Ever since, I have felt guilty, dirty and immoral. I don't know why I should feel this way – I hated it and cried and pleaded for him to go away. Now, even when I see a couple kiss I feel sick. I was a virgin, but now I don't know what I will be able to tell my future husband . . . . At times I'm just so filled with anger I could scream.' MARY

Dear Mary,
We appreciate that you have shared this painful experience with us. You are experiencing feelings which nearly everyone has after such a trauma – feeling shattered by your own vulnerability and helplessness, afraid, angry at having something taken from you by force, and dirty because of the tasteless and violent crime. But you are not damaged property, Mary. Your rape was not a crime of sex or a matter of choice, but a crime of violence committed against you – an unwilling victim. You are not the perpetrator, but a victim.

You say you were a virgin before the rape. You are a virgin still. Virginity is a moral issue. Being or not being a virgin is determined by your choice, and since you had no choice, you still retain your virginity. You are not guilty or immoral, because your will was opposed to the act.

Most women in your situation initially go through a denial stage. They find it impossible to tell anyone and so they try to cope alone. As they begin to admit their feelings of rage, they can, however, begin to feel guilty and depressed. It is not uncommon for them continually to rehearse the experience and blame themselves for exposing themselves to the situation, even though it may have been unavoidable. The end results are the confused feelings you are apparently experiencing.

This is why we would like to suggest a few

opinions and suggestions of our parents. Through all the stumbling that your teenager is going through, you need to know that she or he wants your approval. Parents need to help their children negotiate the stormy waters of these major decisions.

steps which may help you in your recovery:

First, talk to family, friends, and caring people about your feelings. Painful feelings won't go away by being ignored. However, by talking to caring people you will begin to accept and work through the anger and hurt, and return to a normal routine. Reach out for help because you deserve it.

Secondly, emotional flashbacks and panic feelings such as you feel when seeing a couple kiss, are common. You are not stupid or unusual. At such times find someone who can give you reassurance, or think of times when physical closeness to a boyfriend brought pleasant and good feelings.

Thirdly, rape often gives a woman a profound feeling of powerlessness and a sense of loss of control over her life. Allow yourself to move out and make choices as soon as possible so as to restore the sense of control in your life.

Finally, your concern about your future marriage is understandable. While the act of violence may leave some scars, your essential moral self is still the same. You are not damaged property but, rather, you have been the unwilling victim of a crime of violence. Any sensitive and caring husband will understand this.

In the *Focus on the Family's Guide to Growing a Healthy Home*, Dr James Dobson says many parents of adolescents think that their future looks something like this

In actual fact, he says, the reality is more like this

The five messages teens want to hear most
- ❏ 'I'm proud of you!'
- ❏ 'You can always come to me with anything and I'll be there to listen.'
- ❏ 'I understand you' or 'I want to understand.'
- ❏ 'I trust you.'
- ❏ 'I love you!'

There's only one of me
Parents, you can survive your child's stormy years by clinging to the promise of Proverbs 22:6, 'Train up a child in the way he should go, and when he is old he will not depart from it.' (RAV.)

There are two sides to this verse.

If you continually expose your children to negative words that tear down their self-esteem, they'll grow up and 'not depart from it'.

That's why you see a girl with an abusive father end up marrying someone who's just like her dad. That's the only example she has! Our children can only work with the tools we give them. The Bible has a verse which says, 'visiting the iniquity of the fathers upon the children unto the third and fourth generation.' (Exodus 20:5, KJV.) Each parent has a duty to examine himself or herself and announce, 'This destructive family system is going to end with me.'

The tragedy of the sexually-abused child

Please help me. I don't know who to turn to. You might not believe me anyway.

It is hard to believe that such a thing can happen in a Christian family, but it has – to me. As a child of 11 I was sexually abused by a relative, day in and day out, for five years. I got to the place where I hated him.

He was a respected leader in the church, and I just didn't know what to do. All the time I had a kind of loyalty to him, and realized what might happen if I told anyone.

But today I am still deeply hurt. Every so often I go through a bad day and feel dirty, guilty, ashamed. I have tried to forgive and forget, but he doesn't accept it as wrong and has never asked to be forgiven. I feel I can't really get the matter behind me until I have forgiven. How can I when he won't ask?

I needed a 'safe home' to run to then. But even that might have caused trouble by exposing what he had done to me.

Please help me, because you might help another reader too.

I wish your situation was a rare tragedy that occurred only in the most unusual of circumstances. Unfortunately, variations on this theme are increasingly common today. The last line of your letter was a very welcome sight because some of what follows is to be implemented at an earlier stage than you are at right now. Understand that radical problems cannot be solved by pollyanna suggestions. So tighten your seatbelt.

STEP ONE Parents, rescue your child! You must first tell your parents. If the abuser is your father, tell your mother. Tragically, there are women who knowingly

The Hebrew word for 'way' means *bent* or *leaning* or *inclination* or *disposition* or *temperament*. It comes from the same word as a *bow*. Every child has his or her own bent. It is the job of parenthood to adapt one's childrearing practices according to the bent of the child. You hear some parents say: 'I treat all my children the same.' Well, they are not the same, they are unique gifts from God. You may, however, give them all the same unconditional love, but as parents

permit their husbands to abuse their daughters and authorities are never informed. Their right to be called mothers ends right there. Mothers or fathers, if abuse is going on in your home, I plead with you, rescue your child! Risk damaging your marriage, risk destroying it even, but rescue your child! Nothing is so important as your giving your child the opportunity to grow up with a healthy mind and healthy body. Young person, tell your parent or parents and pray God they act.

STEP TWO Get out of the house!
You have stated it well: you needed a 'safe home' to run to. If the home you are in is not a safe one, if no parent is defending you, then get out. I'm serious. There are agencies who can help you. Your developmental years are critical years: they can never be lived over again. The sad truth is that there are some scars that will never be healed. As soon as you feel things are not as they should be, ACT!

STEP THREE Declare yourself 'Not Guilty'!
You feel disgust and revulsion, not just for the relative but for yourself! It is almost as if you have taken the entire blame for the exploitation you suffered. But listen! You must declare yourself 'Not Guilty'! IT IS NOT YOUR FAULT. You are still God's child made in His image. You may not feel it but you've got to believe it. Loving begins with God: 'He first loved us' (1 John 4:19). I can love myself because GOD LOVES ME. You are not a broken person in a whole world; you are a WHOLE person in a broken world. One, God loves you. Two, others believe in you. Three, you respect yourself. That makes you once, twice, THREE TIMES a lady.

Dr. J. O. Brown
Reprinted from *'Encounter'* No.1, 1988

you ought to make a study of your children. Watch them carefully. Your discipline tactics will vary from child to child. Some children react favourably when you praise them: 'Your homework is so neat, now please go and tidy your room.' And off she goes with a smile on her face. Your other child may not react like that. With him a firm, more directive approach may be necessary. It means spending time with them.

Having your cake and icing too
A study was done on businessmen in Chicago to determine how much quality time they spent with their sons. It was discovered that, on average, Chicago businessmen spend six minutes a week in meaningful dialogue with their sons. It is impossible to train up a child in the way he or she should go in just six minutes a week. If you took the time to bear children you ought to take the time to rear them too. Elizabeth Achtemeier puts it this way:

'I sometimes think that children are the gift which is given out of the extravagance of God's grace.

Children are different and, therefore, react differently to both praise and discipline. In consequence parents will have to vary their disciplinary tactics from child to child.

(cf. Genesis 1:28), the final portion which makes our cup run over and magnifies our joy beyond all our original wishing. Children are a marvellous superfluity, the frosting on our cake of matrimonial bliss!'

Look at your children with new eyes, now – they are your icing on the cake!

Children on loan

Samuel's mother, Hannah, prayed for a child. When he was born she declared, 'For this child I prayed;

They are not absolutely necessary to the marital relationship. God fills our cup to the brim with His good gift of a mate for us. Then, on top of that, He adds His marvellous gift of children. They become the overflow of His extravagance, the superabundance of blessing added to His original blessing

PARENTAL EXPECTATIONS

FAIR AND REALISTIC *UNCONDITIONAL LOVE*	UNFAIR AND UNREALISTIC *CONDITIONAL LOVE*
Accepts child's liability.	Expects the child to be a genius.
Helps child to do his best.	Drives child to greater exertion.
Accepts failure, but helps child to understand why he failed and shows how to succeed.	Blames failure on child.
Awards effort.	Awards success.
Works with child's interests and aptitudes.	Forces child to become what parent(s) want(s).
Child is loved for himself.	Strong contrast made between success and failure.
	Child loved for the glory he brings to the family.
	Child feels rejected if he does not bring credit to the family.
Success measured in terms of being a happy, sociable person, achieving at his own level.	Success measured in intellectual or physical prowess.
An ordinary child who is naughty sometimes and sorry sometimes. A very young Christian.	A pious perfect child who behaves like a saint.
Getting dirty, cuts and bruises, torn clothes are part of healthy play.	My child should always be spotless.
A child will act as a child.	The child is judged by adult standards or conduct.
He will pick up some bad language in school, but we will tell him what is suitable language and what is not.	My child would never use words like that.

and the Lord hath given me my petition which I asked of him: therefore also I have lent him to the Lord; as long as he liveth he shall be lent to the Lord.' (1 Samuel 1:27, 28, KJV.) The name Samuel means lent to the Lord. The reason why Hannah could lend her son to God for as long as he lived was that God had lent Samuel to her in the first place, for as long as he would live. Our children do not belong to us, they are ours on loan. We can be protective, we can be possessive, we can be jealous, *only because we have been asked to care for God's property*.

It's all right for our children to bear our image, but first and foremost our children are to bear the image of God. No wonder Jesus said, ' "Let the little children come to me, and do not forbid them." ' (Mark 10:14, RAV.) Woe betide the person who takes advantage of this helpless property of God. We live in an age of rampant child abuse, the majority of it taking place in our own homes. What perpetuates child abuse in the home is what perpetuates spouse abuse; not only the feelings of power and control, but also a misguided sense of ownership. Adult, you've got to recognize that the child does not belong to you; your spouse does not belong to you; and, if you want to know the truth, even *you* yourself don't belong to you! 1 Corinthians 6:18-20 (LB) says:

'That is why I say you should steer clear of sexual immorality. No other sin affects the body as this one does. When you sin in this way it is against your own body.

HEAVEN'S SPECIAL CHILD

SARAH POOTS

A meeting was held far from earth.
'It's time again for another birth,'
Said the angels to the Lord above.
'This special child will need much love.

'Her progress may seem very slow;
Accomplishments she may not show.
And she will require extra care
From the folks she'll meet down there.

'She may not run, laugh or play;
Her thoughts may seem far away.
In many ways she won't adapt,
And she'll be known as handicapped.

'So let's be careful where she's sent;
We want her life to be content.
Please, Lord, find the parents who
Will do this special job for you.

'They will not realize right away
The leading role they're asked to play,
But with this child from above
Comes stronger faith and richer love.

'And soon they'll know the privilege given,
In caring for this gift from heaven
This precious charge, so meek and mild,
Is Heaven's very SPECIAL CHILD.'

Our children are on loan to us – from God.

Haven't you yet learned that your body is the home of the Holy Spirit God gave you, and that he lives within you? Your own body does not belong to you. For God has bought you with a great price. So use every part of your body to give glory back to God, because he owns it.'

So, the children God loans us are special; but some are *extra* special. I like how Charles Swindoll puts it in his book, *You and Your Child:*

'Some children, because of unusual circumstances during the prenatal period or at birth – or afterward – are marked off by the Lord as extremely special gifts: the unplanned child, the adopted child, the disabled child, the gifted child, the hyperactive child, and the one-parent child.'

We were expecting our first baby. The nurse booked my wife into the hospital; something about protein in the urine. She was six months pregnant. She did not feel unwell but they kept her in; something about toxaemia. She was only twenty-seven weeks, but they started to get worried; something about high blood pressure. She had been in a week when I left the hospital on Saturday evening feeling that the doctors were particularly concerned; something about pre-eclampsia. I requested that I be called if there were any developments. I reversed the car into the drive in preparation for an emergency. No phone call came, but before I retired to bed I called the hospital.

'Mrs Brown on Ward 8, please.' There was a pause:

'There's no Mrs Brown on this ward.'

'There must be, I've just left there, please look again.' After a pause,

'No, there's no Mrs Brown here! Let me look if she's gone to the delivery ward.' The nurse checked the list and came back on the line in a matter-of-fact tone.

'Mrs Brown has gone to delivery.'

'And nobody called me?' I screamed incredulously, slamming down the phone. I didn't know what to think, but I suddenly felt so terribly alone. I called my mother-in-law in Bermuda, and Lincoln, my local church elder, then rushed to the hospital. Lincoln and his wife Maureen arrived at the same time as I did. Staff were wheeling a tearful Pattiejean into the delivery room. My elder was overcome. I had called him to comfort me, but I had to comfort him!

We sat down in the waiting room with what seemed to be fathers and grandmothers. After a while an announcement came over the loudspeaker system. 'Mr Smith.' Mr Smith got up, went outside. We heard the nurse speaking to him in hushed tones. Something about them doing all they could. Mr Smith broke down. The next announcement: 'Mr Jones.' Mr Jones went out. 'Stillborn.' We heard Mr Jones break down. A third announcement: 'Mr Brown.' I went out of the room. The nurse said, 'You have a phone call.'

What a relief! It turned out to be my mother-in-law calling the hospital all the way from Bermuda. She had all Pattiejean's sisters gathered together in her living room. They were hanging on to her every word. She called out, 'Has Pattiejean had the baby?'

I looked at the nurse: 'Has Pattiejean had the baby?'

She said, 'Yes.'

I looked down at the phone and said, 'Yes.'

'What is it?'

I looked at the nurse. 'What is it?'

She said, 'It's a girl.'

I said, 'It's a girl.'

'How heavy?'

I looked at the nurse. 'How heavy?'

'One pound thirteen and a half ounces, 840 grams....'

The nurse saw my reaction. 'Would you like to see the baby, Mr Brown?'

I followed her to a part of the hospital we hadn't seen on our pre-natal visits. I saw babies strapped to wires and tubes, flashing lights blinking everywhere. To prepare me for what I was about to see, the nurse said, 'Mr Brown, you have a beautiful baby girl.'

Then I saw her.

Every parent carries a mental picture of what his or her child will look like. What I saw was not my child. What was in front of me was a still, seemingly lifeless foetus attached to tubes and surrounded by anxious medical personnel. 'Would you like me to take a picture of your baby, Mr Brown?' I had scarcely comprehended the reason for the question when it was followed by a hammer blow: 'Would you like the baby baptized?' I knew what she meant. Our baby could die at any moment.

'I don't need any priest,' I retorted. 'I am a minister and I have minister colleagues.'

I called my friend, Pastor Theodore Stewart. When he arrived he called the doctors into the room. He called the nurses into the room. He did not bring holy water. He brought the Holy Bible. He opened it to John 10:10 and read, ' "I have come that they may have life, and that they may have it more abundantly." ' (RAV.)

'What is her situation, doctor?' I asked.

'The first few hours are critical.'

After a few hours: 'How is she doing, doctor?'

'We can't say anything until after twenty-four hours.'

After twenty-four hours: 'Is she going to survive, doctor?'

'We won't know for sure until a week has passed.' Oh, the agony!

But I want you to know that life surged through the veins of that supine body, and from that day, after prayer had been offered, she never looked back. She started to

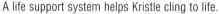

A life support system helps Kristle cling to life.

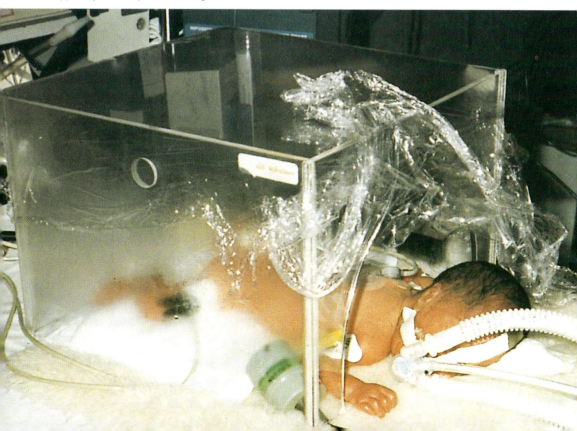

put on weight, shrugged off her prematureness, and is now a bright young lady in high school!

The nurse who had been on duty that day wrote to me: 'I have been asked to give a talk. Could you please send me a picture of your daughter when she was in the incubator strapped to all those tubes? Then could you also send a picture of what she looks like today. Your daughter had a severe case of pulmonary emphysema and we have never seen a baby recover like that.'

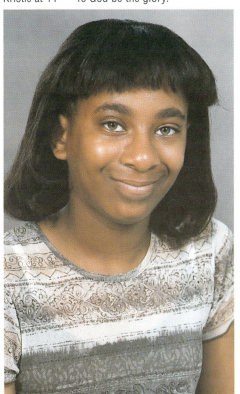

Kristle at 11 — To God be the glory.

'Hallelujah!' I thought.

We decide to call her Kristle. Somebody heard about it and said, 'Oh, Krystal, from *Dynasty*.' I said, 'I'm sorry, I don't understand.'

'You know, Krystal from the *Dynasty* television soap opera, Krystal Carrington.'

I said, 'No! It's Kristle from the German Kristel, which is the equivalent of the English name Christine, which in turn is the feminine form of Christian, which means *follower of Christ*!' They did not ask me any more questions after that. Having had such an experience you cannot name your child after some fake television personality. Kristle was on loan to us but *Kristle belonged to God!*

I think of that when I'm tempted to be harsh towards her. I'm reminded that we almost didn't have her at all. I bought a book by Dan Bolin called, *How to Be Your Daughter's Daddy: 365 Ways to Show Her You Care.* Even though we give marriage and parenting seminars across the world, I still need wisdom from God to help me care for the treasure that God has entrusted us with. It's not all one-way traffic, either. You teach your children, but you also learn from them. They can teach us a thing or two, and sometimes they're not shy in letting us know!

After one less-than-successful discipline session, our son Jamel made a penetrating remark that pierced my soul. I had to write it down. If Jamel lives what he preached that day at the age of 6, I guarantee he'll make a wonderful husband for someone. May it speak to you as it continually speaks to me:

'When I'm a daddy I'm not going to shout at my children or hit them. I'm just going to talk to them and say, "Now you shouldn't do that . . . ." I'm going to love my wife, I'm not going to divorce her, I'm going to kiss her every morning and every night and tell her, "I love you," and sleep with her in the bed.'

Don't lie, don't steal, don't cheat.

Don't embarrass your family; listen to your family; listen to your parents and other responsible adults.

Always do your best and improve on yesterday's work; develop a work attitude.

Learn as much as you can; always expand your knowledge base.

Seek quality in all things rather than weakening quantity.

Always be creative; do not settle for easy answers or conclusions. Think for yourself and learn to be responsible for your decisions.

Learn from mistakes and always oppose that which is not good.

Do homework and housework every day.

Avoid alcohol, drugs and cigarettes.

Respect elders.

What MONTH IS IT THIS Month?

Sometimes we lose track of what's really important in our lives. Have you heard people say, 'Enjoy your children now, they grow up so quickly'? Well, here's a chance to enjoy your time with your children by giving a special focus to each month.

Supervise your children as they match each month with a description – whichever month they like. Suggest ways to make the month meaningful, exciting, and fulfilling.

LOVEWORK ON CHAPTER 7

JANUARY
SMILING MONTH

Try to wake up and come home with a smile on your face. Try to be happy when you come through the front door after a hard day's work, and determine to stay calm no matter what may confront you! Share good, clean, *funny* jokes. Any other ideas?

FEBRUARY
COMPLIMENTING MONTH

Tell your daughter that the dress is pretty because it's on her. Have some of your children's school work laminated. Admire your son's handwriting and the good condition of his toy cars. Praise your daughter during her music practice, school or church plays.

MARCH
READING MONTH

Go to the local library and take out books that were your favourites when you were their age. Take every opportunity you can this month to read with and to your children. Watch less television in order to have more fun reading.

APRIL
SAVING MONTH

Teach your children the value of tithes and offerings; how to reserve a tenth of their allowance for the work of the ministry; and then to give some of their money for those less fortunate. Open a savings account with them and let them contribute regularly. My own experience of savings began when my godly grandmother took me selling Christian literature as a little boy of 6 and opened a savings account for me with my earnings!

MAY
SPENDING MONTH

Look through a toy catalogue with them, and take your children to the shops they like; guide them in spending their allowance on things they have saved up for and had their eye on for some time; then ask them to select one of their toys that is in good working order to give to charity. Let your daughter get that skirt or those shoes that *she* likes.

JUNE
HOLIDAY MONTH

Go on a train ride together. Once a year my brother Michael and his wife Sandria go with their excited children Danielle and Jason to collect holiday brochures, and the children actually select the family holiday.

JULY
HELPING MONTH

Help your children tidy their room, clean up after their pet. Ask them to help you wash the car, wash the dishes, etc., but especially this month focus on others. Help a senior citizen with their garden or their shopping. Sponsor a needy child and have the children write them a letter.

AUGUST
GAMES MONTH

Michelle and Bobby made an announcement that their home was

open for games, and over forty people came! Play some family games and invite others to join you. Play games that require thinking. Children, what are your favourite games?

SEPTEMBER
FOOD MONTH

This month cook especially those dishes that the children enjoy. Make some special treats for them. Have them bake with you, with or without a recipe. Plan to eat out once a week this month. Any ideas where, children?

OCTOBER
TOGETHERNESS MONTH

Watch some family videos together, look at photograph albums, tell your children stories about when you were their age, visit a children's museum, go to a sports event, learn the names of your daughter's dolls or stuffed animals. Together, write a family newspaper for friends and relatives.

NOVEMBER
INTIMACY MONTH

Psychologists say we need twelve hugs a day in order to be emotionally healthy. Do your best this month! Parents, kiss each other in your children's presence – our children need to see that their parents love each other; and they love watching it!

DECEMBER
HEART-TUNING MONTH

Keep the family spiritually in tune. Ideas: Make sure everybody has a Bible. Help them to learn the books of the Bible. Watch Christian movies and gospel music videos. Have sentence prayers for ten minutes. Sing, sing, sing!

8 You can love again

'For a brother who has a non-Christian wife who is willing to live with him he should not divorce her. A wife in a similar position should not divorce her husband. For the unbelieving husband is, in a sense, consecrated by being joined to the person of his wife; the unbelieving wife is similarly "consecrated" by the Christian brother she has married. If this were not so then your children would bear the stains of paganism, whereas they are actually consecrated to God. But if the unbelieving partner decides to separate, then let there be a separation. The Christian partner need not consider himself bound in such cases.... A woman is bound to her husband while he is alive, but if he dies she is free to marry whom she likes – but let her be guided by the Lord.'
(1 CORINTHIANS 7:12-15, 39, JBP.)

No one is immune

'London is a bad place to have a wife.' That was the opening sentence K. D. Djan wrote in his article in the *New African* which he entitled, 'Till London Do Us Part'.

'London is a bad place to have a wife,' wrote K. D. Djan in an article in *New African* entitled 'Till London Do Us Part'.

At least 40 per cent of UK marriages will end in divorce, the highest figure for any European Union country. Christians of African descent in the West are affected by this trend. Djan goes on to say, 'Marriage was once said to be for life. Not any more. The more Africans abroad absorb Western ideas, the more their marriages break up. From Germany to America, the story is the same. In Britain, the African community is in virtual crisis as their marriages break up all around them.'

Pastor Donald McFarlane, in the *Christian Post*, echoes the same thought from a Caribbean perspective:

'Have West Indians gained more than they have lost by coming to Britain? This is a question

At least 40 per cent of UK marriages will end in divorce. The UK now has the highest divorce rate of any European Union country.

frequently asked by many West Indians as they analyse their experience since leaving the shores of their native islands to reside in the "motherland". From seventeen years of observation as a church pastor and administrator, my conclusion is that these historically-ambitious and Bible-loving people have probably lost more than they have gained by exchanging the blue skies of the Caribbean for the grey days of Britain. This loss is most conspicuous in the area of family values.'

Divorce
Scripture does not recommend divorce. We acknowledge the reality and prevalence of divorce as a tragic departure from God's ideal and couples should do all in their power to save their marriages. The acute feeling of loneliness is often all-consuming at this time. The extended family and community of faith must support couples in crisis, for 'if one member (of the body) suffers all the other members suffer with it'. (1 Corinthians 12:26, JBP.) While *communication* (1 Corinthians 7:3-5), *compatibility* (2 Corinthians 6:14) and *commitment* (1 Corinthians 7:10, 11) characterize the solution or strengthening of marriages, *adultery* (Matthew 5:32), *abuse* (1 Corinthians 6:9) and *abandonment* (1 Corinthians 7:15) characterize the dissolution of the same.

Unfaithfulness to the marriage vow has generally been seen to mean adultery and/or fornication. However, the New Testament word for fornication includes certain other irregularities (1 Corinthians 6:9; 1 Timothy 1:9, 10; Romans 1:24-27). Therefore, sexual perversions, including homosexual practices, are also recognized as a misuse of sexual powers and a violation of the divine intention in marriage.

Even though the Scriptures allow divorce for the reasons mentioned above, earnest endeavours should be made by those concerned to effect a reconciliation, urging the innocent spouse to forgive the guilty one and the latter to amend his or her conduct, so that the marriage union may be maintained. In the event that reconciliation is not effected, the innocent spouse has the biblical right to secure a divorce, and also to remarry.

If first marriages are traumatic, subsequent marriages may be even more so. Every marriage brings with it baggage, from a painful childhood or unhappy adolescence to disappointment in adulthood. In subsequent marriages the difficulties of the first marriage may be compounded.

There are five issues of which

those in or entering into a subsequent marriage should be aware:

❏ *The possibility of unmourned former relationships.*

The reality is that so much of the past exists in the present. All kinds of feelings may surface when you least expect them: guilt, betrayal, jealousy, resentment, inadequacy, helplessness, selfishness, fear, confusion, anxiety and depression. The most remarkable aspect of many troubled second marriages is the degree to which one or both partners are still actively and intensely engaged in dialogue with their previous partner. It may well be that the 'leaving' has not been fully completed before the 'cleaving' has taken place; it may be that it never will be.

❏ *Possible difficulties in establishing a committed second relationship.*

It does not always come 'naturally' second time around. The novelty can wear off more quickly than the first time. The honeymoon period may not last as long. It does not mean there is no love there. It simply means that couples have to work harder to develop it. A subsequent marriage is not merely an ending and a new beginning but often a fusion of the two, at times

Children from different parents have to learn to get on with each other or they will grow up into socially dysfunctional adults.

confusing, disappointing and exhausting.

❑ *Blending the children of one relationship with the children of another.*
Not only do the children have to learn to get on with each other, but the children often receive new directives on how to relate to the absent parent. One man forbade his own children ever to talk about their natural mother in front of their stepmother and stepsiblings. He also forbade his stepchildren to see their natural father. Such behaviour can cause untold agony.

❑ *The danger of comparing the worst of the present situation with the best of the former one.*
Couples have to work on residual feelings they may have about their ex-partners, loss, comparisons, and grieving past successes and failures. It is not uncommon for remarried people to be distressed on hearing that their former spouse is now remarrying. Happy memories come flooding back and the spouse conceals these reactions from his or her partner for fear of provoking anger or distress.

❑ *The negative attitudes of people close to you.*
Some children are very happy when a parent gets married again, others are resentful. There is pain on both sides.

The good news is that for many the second marriage is a blessing. It provides them a new lease of life. Often they have had their hearts crushed by the unkindness of those who do not think they should have remarried, but their remarriage has given them a new lease of life. It has revived their faith in humanity. The sky is blue once more. The birds are singing once again. *We must be happy for these people.* Christopher Compston wrote in his book *Recovering from Divorce:*

Remarriage may give those damaged by divorce a new lease of life.

'What can the Church do about this? It must face up to the reality that divorce, like AIDS, is not going to go away. Both scourges originate from sin but, although God tells us to hate sin, He equally tells us to love the sinner. For too long the Church has viewed the divorced as second-hand citizens even when they are or have become members of the Church.'

So what can be done to prevent marital breakdown?

❏ I believe we need to *recognize the importance of premarital counselling.* Somebody said a little common sense could prevent many divorces but far more marriages. Pastors must come to the place where they refuse to marry couples whom they deem incompatible (Amos 3:3) or unequally yoked (2 Corinthians 6:14). Pastors must also stop this habit of marrying people who come to them a week before the wedding. Each premarital counsellor must establish a minimum time limit which will give him or her adequate time to conduct meaningful premarital counselling.

Some individuals feel that premarital counselling doesn't work because the couples are too blindly in love to listen with sufficient reason. Other counsellors have opted for '*post*-marital counselling', addressing the couple

AUTOBIOGRAPHY
IN FIVE CHAPTERS
PORTIA NELSON

ONE
As I walk down the street,
There is a deep hole in the sidewalk.
I fall in.
I am lost . . . I am hopeless.
It isn't my fault.
It takes forever to find a way out.

TWO
I walk down the same street.
There is a deep hole in the sidewalk.
I pretend I don't see it.
I fall in again.
I can't believe I'm in the same place.
But it isn't my fault.
It still takes a long time to get out.

THREE
I walk down the same street.
There is a deep hole in the sidewalk.
I see it is there.
I still fall in . . . It's a habit.
My eyes are open.
I know where I am.
It is MY FAULT.
I get out immediately.

FOUR
I walk down the same street.
There is a deep hole in the sidewalk.
I walk round.

FIVE
I walk down another street . . .

Goals of a marital and premarital relationships weekend

- ✳ To present the Christian institution of marriage as a realistic and positive lifestyle.
- ✳ To provide an opportunity for each couple to experience spiritual unity.
- ✳ To provide participants with the experience and opportunity for personal growth.
- ✳ To allow the couples to explore their commitment to each other.
- ✳ To facilitate communication between the couple.
- ✳ To assist the couple in planning their marriage as opposed to just planning their wedding.
- ✳ To provide the atmosphere and the time for the couple to reflect and share together.

shortly after the wedding. It is certainly advisable to have a meeting with the couple shortly after the wedding or honeymoon. The real benefit of premarital counselling, however, extends far beyond any questionnaire which may be distributed, video the couple may see, or advice which may be given. The real value lies *in the relationship which is established between the pastoral counsellor and the couple,* so that when trouble strikes, the couple will remember those special sessions together and go to him or her for help.

❑ Not only do we need to emphasize the importance of premarital counselling, but we need *to emphasize that marriage is for life.* Marriage is based on promises. It's a case of, 'Pray for what you want and live with what you get.' Marriage is for keeps! In the book, *Letters to Young Lovers,* Ellen White says:

'If men and women are in the habit of praying twice a day before they contemplate marriage, they should pray four times a day when such a step is anticipated. If ever the Bible is needed as a counsellor,

it is before taking a step that binds persons together for life.'
❏ Attend a marriage enrichment or intimacy-for-life weekend. These 'Marriage Enrichment' programmes allow for sharing in small group settings. 'Marriage Encounter' weekends are quite intimate with all sharing done privately between each couple. 'Marriage Commitment' seminars blend the two. You may say, 'I don't have a bad marriage, so why should I go?' These seminars are designed to make a good marriage better. A spouse may insist, 'Well, I don't need such a programme.' Your marriage may not need one, but your marriage surely deserves one.

One stark reality is that things can go wrong in your marriage, as they have in others. Recognize that it is no weakness to go for help, whether within the extended family or to a relationships counsellor. Perhaps one of the cruellest games is played by the marriage partner who says, 'If you want to go for counselling, it's up to you, but don't involve me.' Even if you have to go alone, however, you can still benefit. The unbelieving spouse can be won over by the caring concern of a Christian spouse (1 Corinthians 7:14).

Sandra Finley Doran's book, *Every Time I Say Grace We Fight,* reminds us that, in the final analysis, the salvation of our spouse is ultimately God's business. Therefore, go to Him. I like how Dr Albert Waite puts it in the *Cornerstone* journal:

'The heavenly Counsellor will spend time with you, give you all the attention you need, respect you with no reservations. He is both Counsellor and Comforter. His service to you is a gift. Free. He confirms His long-term commitment to your eternal well-being when He says: "And surely [I am telling you the truth] I will be with you always [His involvement is not temporary], to the very end of the age." (Matthew 28:20, NIV.)'

Widowhood

Bereavement is always painful; but

No kind of loss matches the loss of a husband or a wife.

no loss matches that of a husband or wife, 'bone of my bones, and flesh of my flesh.' (Genesis 2:23, KJV.) It is normal for the partner to experience shock, anger and numbness; there may be times and public periods of mourning. Death, though tragic, is recognized as a part of the life cycle. This is very healthy. In many Western societies, unfortunately, death is a taboo subject and people bottle up their grief.

Pastoral counsellors, friends and family members, visit as soon as you can. Don't worry about what to say. Go to listen, but try to talk about the person who has died and get the spouse to talk about his or her partner. Be aware that each person is an individual with his

STAGES OF GRIEF

DESCENDING   ASCENDING

DISBELIEF   ASSIMILATION
            ACCEPTANCE
DISORGANIZATION
            AGGRESSION
   DENIAL
DEPRESSION   ANXIETY
      GUILT

Visit the bereaved. Don't worry about what to say; listen as the bereaved person talks about the person who has died.

when you wonder if you are not going mad. Guilt, loneliness, denial, bargaining, and depression may all occur before acceptance. While the process of grief can go on for two years and more, the memories will last a lifetime.

African societies allow for grief to be expressed and shared by the community. There are extended

Each person will have his or her own grieving pattern. Never say, 'Pull yourself together,' or 'I'm sure you'll manage.'

or her own grieving pattern. Empathize and give unconditional positive regard by valuing the person without judging him or her. Do not say, 'Pull yourself together', or 'I'm sure you'll manage.' Be aware of the continual need for practical help. Remember birthdays and special anniversaries and, above all, continue to be there with love and encouragement.

To the bereaved I say, life is God's gift to you; don't give up on it. Allow yourself to weep freely. Accept that death has happened and determine now to look to the future. Forgive and forget. Replace negative thoughts with positive ones. Recognize that your marriage covenant has ended. Remarriage may eventually be the right step, but don't hurry it. Be considerate towards your relatives and friends. Look for ways to help others. You can make it. Reach out and touch somebody's hand; make the world a better place if you can. Oh, and by the way, make sure you cook for yourself and eat properly – you are worth it. God will give you a new lease of life, believe it!

Overcoming temptation
As we consider traumas in the relationship, I leave you with three thoughts.

1 What happened to one person can happen to you.
This pilgrimage which we call marriage can at times be so lonely that we find ourselves unable even to speak to our spouse about worries, fears, and temptations towards unfaithfulness. Some people think that by talking about it we are actually increasing the chances of it happening. Nothing could be farther from the truth. J. Allen Petersen wrote a book called *The Myth of the Greener Grass,* and, in it, he says that the first step towards preventing an affair is to acknowledge that it can actually happen – to *you.*

In her commentary on Samson, Ellen White wrote in *Patriarchs and Prophets,* 'Those who in the way of duty are brought into trial may be sure that God will preserve them; but if men wilfully place themselves under the power of temptation, they will fall, sooner or later.' The story of Samson, the world's strongest man, was recorded in Scripture so that no person should ever say, 'I am

Loneliness within marriage can lead to affairs particularly in the workplace.

THE SEVEN DEADLY STEPS

- ❏ Has some stagnancy crept into your life work?
- ❏ Do you find yourself increasingly wondering, Is it really worth it?
- ❏ Do you find yourself having lingering doubts about your marital compatibility?
- ❏ Are you experiencing disillusionment with your marriage, almost to breaking point?
- ❏ Does the grass seem greener on the other side of the fence?
- ❏ Are you prepared to recognize the possibility of sexual indiscretion?
- ❏ Are you bottling up your frustration with nobody aware of your inner turmoil?

strong enough not to fall . . . .' Why not take the time to examine yourself right now?

2 *What happened to one person has not increased its chances of happening to you.*

Some people think that because one person's marriage has broken down, perhaps somebody close to them, it has somehow increased the odds of their marriage being in trouble. A type of paranoia begins to creep into the relationship. A book was written about the great responsibilities of parenting today, as well as the awesome possibilities of failure, and it was entitled *Parents on the Run*. The idea was that the whole thing is so out of control today that parents are literally on the run. It concluded that this did not necessarily have to be your scenario.

Don't get panicky. The sun is still in the sky. God is still in control. You've got to affirm for yourself that, 'His eye is still on the sparrow and I know he watches me.' *Patriarchs and Prophets* continues the lessons from Samson:

'The very ones whom God purposes to use as His instruments for a special work, Satan employs His utmost power to lead astray. He attacks us at our weak points, working through defects in the character to gain control of the whole man; and he knows if these defects are cherished he will succeed. *But none need be overcome.* Man is not left alone to conquer the power of evil by his own feeble efforts. Help is at hand and will be given to every soul who really desires it. Angels of God, that ascend and descend the ladder which Jacob saw in vision, will help every soul who will, to climb even to the highest heaven.'

It need not happen to you. And then finally,

3 *What God has done for others He can do for you*.

I'm so glad that 'if we confess our sins, he is faithful and just to forgive us our sins and to cleanse us from all unrighteousness'! That means that *no matter what I may have done,* God looks at me as if I had never fallen. Others may have

It's a matter of keeping the flame alive

Sol Gordon, psychologist, was once asked what were the most important elements of a marriage relationship. He found the following top ten characteristics which are presented here.

1 LAUGHTER
Situations are often turned from molehills into mountains simply because a sense of humour is lacking. Whether or not you rise above the difficulty or let it tear you apart, to a large extent depends on your ability to see the humour and laugh at yourself.

2 FRIENDSHIPS
Most couples have some friends whom they enjoy together, and they also have some whom they enjoy separately. This is normal, healthy, and even necessary. Couples who expect to meet each other's social needs in full may find that their relationship will begin to feel confined and boring. The slightest interest in others is seen as an act of 'unfaithfulness'. Such jealousy arises from a fear of being left out or of losing love. Just as each spouse is a separate individual with different interests, abilities in work, hobby or sporting activities, so too there will be a social circle which forms in association with these acttivies and which need not be seen as a threat to love.

3 INVOLVEMENT
That which gives meaning and purpose to our lives are those things to which we are committed. Couples often find this sense of purpose both inside and outside the marriage and home, for example, church, sporting clubs, etc. Mutual involvement in various activities and causes builds a sense of partnership.

4 SEX
Sexual fulfilment is an expression of shared intimacy. In order to be fulfilling, sex needs loving with it. Too many couples become blasé in their sexual relationship so that it becomes humdrum. Sex is a part of marriage, but for some couples it is quite overrated as the main benefit of marriage.

5 SHARING
Friendship is a mutual relationship of honest give and take. To share is to give oneself to the other by spending time and doing things together. Deeper friendships

a problem with that, but Jesus doesn't! If I understand my Bible correctly, cleansed means washed, and Revelation 22:14 (NIV) says, ' "Blessed are those who *wash* their robes, that they may have the right to the tree of life and may go through the gates into the city." ' (Emphasis ours.) The next verse actually mentions the sexually immoral, but says they are *outside* the city. Thank God! As long as I confess, I'm no longer part of that group. He cleaned up David and He cleaned up Solomon. 'It is no secret what God can do, what He's done for others He'll do for you.'

involve a level of vulnerability as each shares something of themselves with the other in delicate trust.

6 INTEGRITY
The word 'phoney' is derived from an old British colloquialism used by thieves for something which is false, fake or counterfeit. For a trust relationship to develop, each must be genuine and trustworthy.

7 TALK
That which fosters the growth of normal relationships also nurtures the romantic relationship. Communication is much more than just talking. Communication is a process of keeping in touch so that each knows what thoughts and feelings the other is experiencing. The more we know of each other, the deeper will be our level of understanding, caring and, consequently, the more fulfilling and lasting will be the friendship.

8 LOVE
Love is a feeling of deep concern and commitment to another person. To fulfil this commitment the individual will find tangible ways to provide for the needs of that person.

9 ADAPTABILITY
Involves acceptance of the other person's individuality as he or she is, without endeavouring to make carbon copies of oneself. It means allowing the other person to do and be other than exactly what you expect.

10 TOLERANCE
Tolerance is not merely reluctantly putting up with an undesirable person. Tolerance is acceptance – accepting the other's quirks, failings, and disagreeable moods, thus allowing your partner to be human – just as you are.

LOVEWORK ON CHAPTER 8
LOOK AFTER YOURSELF

'Dear Dr Brown,' began a letter I received some time ago, 'It is time for you to have a full dental examination. Your dental team firmly believe in preventative dentistry. If we are able to prevent gum disease and tooth decay, we can ensure that you have a healthy mouth for life. The system has been fully computerized. We can now offer state-of-the-art dental care, from implants to replacing missing teeth, to cosmetic dentistry to restore your smile and confidence.'

Well, dear reader, it's time for you to have a *Total Marriage* examination. The authors of this book firmly believe in preventative marriage. If we are able to prevent helplessness and hopelessness, we believe you have a healthy marriage for life. The social readjustment rating scale has been fully tested cross-culturally. We can now identify some of the major *causes* of stress, some of the major *effects* of stress, and techniques for *managing* stress. If you can learn to recognize (and as far as possible anticipate) a life event, and determine ahead of time to face it together, then we believe that God can restore your smile and confidence. Add up the value of Life Crisis Units for life events experienced in a two-year period and use the scale below to evaluate your marital stress. Please see a minister or Christian counsellor if you find yourself in a continual state of depression and despair.

STRESS AND ILLNESS LIFE CRISIS UNITS

FAMILY

Death of a spouse	100 _____
Divorce	73 _____
Marital separation	65 _____
Death of close family member	63 _____
Marriage	50 _____
Marital reconciliation	45 _____
Major change in health of family	44 _____
Pregnancy	40 _____
Addition of new family member	39 _____
Major change in arguments with mate	35 _____
Son or daughter leaving home	29 _____
In-law troubles	29 _____
Wife starting or ending work	26 _____
Major change in family get-togethers	15 _____
TOTAL	_____

PERSONAL

Detention in gaol	63 _____
Major personal injury or illness	53 _____
Sexual difficulties	39 _____
Death of close friend	37 _____
Outstanding personal achievement	28 _____
Start or end of formal schooling	26 _____
Major change in living conditions	25 _____
Major revision of personal habits	24 _____
Changing to a new school	20 _____
Change in residence	20 _____
Major change in recreation	19 _____
Major change in church activities	19 _____
Major change in social activities	18 _____
Major change in sleeping habits	16 _____
Major change in eating habits	15 _____
Holiday	13 _____
Christmas	12 _____
Minor violations of the law	11 _____
TOTAL	_____

WORK

Being fired from work	47 _____
Retirement from work	45 _____
Major business adjustment	39 _____
Changing to a different line of work	36 _____
Major change in work responsibilities	29 _____
Trouble with boss	23 _____
Major change in working conditions	20 _____
TOTAL	_____

FINANCIAL

Major change in financial state	38 _____
Mortgage or loan over £50,000	31 _____
Mortgage foreclosure	30 _____
Mortgage or loan less than £50,000	17 _____
TOTAL	_____
GRAND TOTAL	_____

EVALUATION:
0 - 150   No significant stress-related health problems
150 - 199   Mild life crisis (33 per cent chance of illness)
200 - 299   Moderate life crisis (50 per cent chance of illness)
300 or over Major life crisis (80 per cent chance of illness)

Children are great fun; they are also the source of considerable stress.

9 'As I have loved you'

'Live lives worthy of your high calling. Accept life with humility and patience, making allowances for each other because you love each other. Make it your aim to be at one in the Spirit, and you will inevitably be at peace with one another.'
(EPHESIANS 4:1-3, JBP.)

'Having loved his own which were in the world, he loved them unto the end.'
(JOHN 13:1, KJV.)

Some years ago I attended my younger sister's wedding. I remember the minister posing the question, 'In an age such as ours, and in a time such as this, why should two people decide to get married?' I thought it was a good question then; I know it is a good question now. What do people really see in marriage?

Communication, compatibility, or commitment?

I used to wonder which was most important, considering the 3 C's of marriage – *communication, compatibility,* and *commitment.* All important ingredients, but which is the most enduring? I started to think. Books have been written with titles such as *Communication: Key to Your Marriage.* But I've known couples well able to communicate, call each other up on the phone, even go out to a restaurant together – years after the divorce! Communication skills, in and of themselves, didn't save the marriage.

What about compatibility? The courts grant divorces on the grounds of incompatibility. Yet Charles and Barbara Snyder wrote a book and called it *Incompatibility: Grounds for a Great Marriage!* They spoke from their own experiences as 'opposites' married for more than thirty years. They said that differences in temperament can actually enhance marital intimacy, once couples are aware and prepared. So that just leaves commitment.

You can have all the communication and compatibility you want, but if you're not committed it's worth nothing. Then, on the other hand, you may go through dry deserts in your communication experience. You may at times doubt

your compatibility, but if you are committed, then you can make it! No wonder Dietrich Bonhoffer said, 'It is not love that sustains the marriage but, from now on, the marriage that sustains your love.'

Commitment, however, is not easy. Neither is it free. It will cost you something. The Bible says Jesus was committed to His disciples, and through them to the world. And John 13:1 says, 'Having loved his own that were in the world, he loved them unto the end.' That's commitment in action. It cost Jesus His life. Perhaps we can say that Christian marriage is characterized by three commit-

Ten ways husbands can say, 'I love you.'

APPLAUD her achievements – daily.
PRAISE her and tell her you love her.
PROVIDE time off to relax and get away.
REACH into your wallet when it's not her birthday.
EAT your own cooking sometimes.

APPRECIATE

CALL her during worktime to say you miss her.
INTEREST yourself in her interests.
ARGUE only when you are by yourselves.
TELL no one about her shortcomings.
EXAMINE her strengths and be blessed by them.

ments. Firstly, an exclusive commitment.

Exclusive commitment
Christian marriage is characterized by an exclusive commitment to each other; 'to forsake all others', 'to keep thee only unto her or him, so long as you both shall live.'

Here is the first prerequisite for faithfulness in marriage: letting our partner know that he or she is the centre of our hearts. That he or she has that reserved spot. That he or she is the most important person in our lives, and will always be treated as such.

It is important to tell our mate in words, every day through the years, that he or she is our most intimate and valued companion. And will never be replaced, no matter how attractive or understanding or compatible some other acquaintance may be.

It is important that our mates see that we will never enter into other relationships that would destroy the intimacy we have with them. And exclusive commitment in marriage is not limited to the sexual sphere.

Intimacy is not only sexual, it is emotional, and intellectual. It arises from values shared and work done together. It is deepened by crises faced and overcome in partnership. And while we are not to cut ourselves off from other people, we must maintain a sacred circle around our marriage, the beloved spouse with whom we are joined in the unity of one flesh by God. It is important for our mates to know that we will never let ourselves continue in some experience with another person which would replace or jeopardize our primary

SEVEN IMPORTANT
THINGS TO SAY IN YOUR MARRIAGE

THE SIX MOST IMPORTANT WORDS
'I admit I made a mistake.'

THE FIVE MOST IMPORTANT WORDS
'You did a good job.'

THE FOUR MOST IMPORTANT WORDS
'What is your opinion?'

THE THREE MOST IMPORTANT WORDS
'I forgive you.'

THE TWO MOST IMPORTANT WORDS
'Thank you.'

THE MOST IMPORTANT WORD
'We.'

THE LEAST IMPORTANT WORD
'I.'

---

loyalty to our mates.

Other people are not to enjoy the central place in our hearts. That is reserved for the nearest and dearest. So devote time to each other. Leave some of those meetings alone. That's right! A juvenile court judge was asked by several members of a women's club what they could do to combat delinquency. Without hesitation the judge replied, 'Stay home.' There are dozens of community or church committee meetings each year which will rob you of valuable time with your spouse. Someone has said that a committee is nothing more than a collection of the unfit, chosen from the unwilling, by the incompetent, to

Barriers to communication

LACK OF COURAGE.
A basic reason behind the reluctance of husbands and wives to discuss innermost problems is fear of criticism. They fear that conversation, by becoming more real, will open wounds to which they are especially sensitive. Aware of his own sense of failure and to protect himself, a husband will often denounce his wife's shortcomings (and vise versa)! This accounts for the mutual recrimination which so often develops in phase two of a marriage, when the 'phase' syndrome has set in.

THE INABILITY TO PUT FEELINGS INTO WORDS.
Because of background or education many are accustomed to articulating what is going on inside of them. Equally, because of background, or limitations in education – or because of an introverted personality – an individual or a couple may find it very difficult to find the right words actually to express the turmoil, hurt or chaos going on inside their minds. In this situation 'communication' too often means rowing. If a couple or one partner has this problem then they are in with a handicap; but the handicap is also a challenge. However falteringly, and however difficult they may find it, they must struggle for the words – and speak them kindly, awaiting patiently the other's response. Good quarrels resolve conflicts while bad ones tear each participant down, leaving more hurt feelings and matters to fight over. It is possible for two people to engage in heated and even noisy discussions where they argue without hurting each other. They stick to the subject with the view to finding a mutually satisfying resolution.

THE FEAR OF RECEIVING GLIB ADVICE.
A husband tells his wife about a problem at work which is deeply troubling him. The wife gives her husband a trite, unthought-through reply: 'Sack your partner! Stand up for yourself or he'll trample all over you! How many times have I told you?' The husband is crushed. The wife does not realize the complexity of the problems he faces. She may think him incompetent.

do the unnecessary. So don't compromise on your regular time together. Keep your marriage special, for not only is marriage an exclusive commitment, Christian marriage is an accepting commitment as well.

Accepting commitment
We've got to learn to accept each other, faults and all. Every married person has to put up with traits and actions on the part of a mate which are at best disagreeable and at worst embarrassing. In the typical marriage, there are lots of petty irritations and dislikes. The committed marriage is one in which we learn to accept, in love, our partner's imperfections, even when

'ASSASSINATE THE SPOUSE.'
This barrier to communication is highlighted by Dr James Dobson. In this destructive game the player (usually the husband) attempts to punish his wife by ridiculing and embarrassing her in front of friends. Bonus points are awarded if he can reduce her to tears; 'These eggs could have been used to pave the Yellow Brick Road. . . .'

THE MONOLOGUER.
This is the person who always insists on having the last word – as well as being a compulsive talker – and as such is a one-person handicap in the communication stakes.

BOTTLING EMOTION.
Conversely, the tendency to feel that it is correct to bottle emotion in silence and hide it behind a poker face is very damaging to the marriage (as well as to physical, mental and spiritual health). Some marriage guidance counsellors say that the 'silent husband' lies behind half of the troubled marriages they encounter. Silence bleeds the life from a marriage as by some haemorrhage.

they lose hair and gain weight.

It's a tremendous thing to feel accepted. That's why so many people in England have dogs. They come home and, no matter if they are early or late, sour or dour, humpy or grumpy, that dog is going to jump all over them, lick their faces, saying, 'It's great to see you, anyhow!' So men, when the dinner's not quite ready or the pie is a little bit burned, kiss her and say, 'It's great to see you, anyhow!' When she comes in a little late and she has not called ahead of time and you got stuck with the housework, kiss her and say, 'It's great to see you, anyhow!' When she wakes up in the morning with curlers in her hair and that nocturnal odour on her lips, kiss her and say, 'It's great to see you, anyhow!'

This is an accepting commitment. It is a commitment which covers and accepts the past. *Even things that happened in past relationships*. It is a commitment based not upon feelings but upon an act of the will. Perhaps, finally, married couples should possess not only an *accepted* commitment, not only an *exclusive* commitment, but also an *anticipating* commitment.

Anticipating commitment
An anticipating commitment anticipates that God has much to do with us yet. The apostle John says,

> '**I will be with you,** *no matter what happens to us or between us. If you should become blind tomorrow, I will be there. If you achieve no success and attain no status in our society, I will be there. When we argue and are angry, as we inevitably will, I will work to bring us together. When we seem totally at odds and neither of us is having our needs fulfilled, I will persist in trying to understand and in trying to restore our relationship. When our marriage seems utterly sterile and going nowhere at all, I will believe that it can work and I will want it to work, and I will do my part to make it work. And when all is wonderful and we are happy, I will rejoice over our life together, and continue to strive to keep our relationship growing and strong. Christ has promised us, "I am with you always, even to the end of the age." Christians in marriage take upon themselves that same unreserved commitment.'*
>
> ELIZABETH ACHTEMEIER, THE COMMITTED MARRIAGE.

YOUR COMMUNICATION STYLE

Ask the following questions about yourself and your spouse and compare your results by circling: Yes (Y), No (N), Sometimes (S).

1. Am I the kind of person who will support and encourage the self-esteem of family members?   Y N S
2. Do I use vague and passive means of expressing feelings through methods such as pouting, sarcasm, nagging, etc?   Y N S
3. Am I aware of, and do I express my feelings, and encourage the free expression of feelings from others?   Y N S
4. Do I tend to be judgemental and harshly critical of others, blaming them for their inadequacies?   Y N S
5. Do I avoid taking personal responsibility by saying: 'That's me, I can't change', 'I can't help myself', or blame circumstances or others for how I feel or act?   Y N S
6. Do I make room for others to express themselves?   Y N S
7. Do I tend to be hostile and aggressive in getting my way?   Y N S
8. Am I honest about admitting a mistake even when it's embarrassing?   Y N S
9. I tend to 'put my best foot forward' when together with others.   Y N S
10. I listen accurately and sympathetically.   Y N S
11. I feel that my friends often misunderstand what I am saying.   Y N S
12. There are things in my life about which I cannot talk, even to my closest and most trusted friend.   Y N S
13. I find it easy to talk rationally even when stressed or angry.   Y N S
14. I share openly with my friends even those things which may put me in a bad light.   Y N S
15. I feel free to confide almost everything to my partner or close friends.   Y N S
16. I get impatient with people who want to talk about their problems.   Y N S
17. I tend to misread what other people mean by what they say.   Y N S
18. My mind tends to wander while others are talking.   Y N S
19. I'm thinking of what I am going to say when listening to someone else.   Y N S
20. I tend to talk a lot about my hobby-horses.   Y N S
21. I tend to lose my temper quickly and/or become over-emotional.   Y N S
22. I find it difficult to see things from another's point of view.   Y N S
23. I have been accused of sending conflicting messages.   Y N S

PRESCRIPTION FOR DULL MARRIAGE SYNDROME

Take a few minutes to think back to your courting days. A pencil and paper will be useful.

❑ Jot down what it was that attracted you to your husband or wife. What was it you liked so much about her face, figure or hair; his features, expresssion or physique?

❑ Make a few notes about personality. Was she vivacious and extrovert? Did you like his quiet confidence? It could be that your partner was coy and shy and you liked to feel protective; maybe he or she was full of fun: a buoyant, happy, infectious sort of person.

❑ List the sorts of things you enjoyed doing together. Maybe it was parties or driving, water-skiing or walking; going to concerts or visiting that special restaurant.

❑ Remember the things your partner did or said which made you happy or gave you pleasure. This could include little gifts, ways and expressions by which you felt loved and wanted. It may also have been a certain touch, a facial expression or things said and whispered.

❑ Remember the ways you used to express your love with words and actions. There were also times when you purposefully plotted a surprise, sent a special card or arranged for a treat.

What worked then will work now.

'Beloved, we are God's children now; it does not yet appear what we shall be.' (See 1 John 3:2.) When God is working His purpose out in our lives, we cannot expect our mate to remain the same. Each of us must see the sign our partner wears every day, which says, 'Please be patient with me, God has not finished with me yet.' God will work with you both, shaping your lives in new ways through new experiences.

It doesn't matter how long you've been married, you've got some exciting days ahead. Don't be surprised by change. Even after

you have been married for twenty-five years, if you think you know everything there is to know about your spouse it's because you haven't been paying attention. If you just watch each other carefully you will see that you have, in fact, married a mystery! There's always something hidden, something new, something difference, something that you're always fascinated with and anxious to learn more about. Put God first, and watch Him do a new thing in you. Temple Gairdner wrote a prayer in his diary just before his marriage:

'That I may come near to her, draw me nearer to Thee than to her;

'That I may know her, make me to know Thee more than her.

'That I may love her with the perfect love of a perfectly whole heart, cause me to love Thee more than her most of all.

'That nothing may be between me and her, be thou between us, every moment. That we may be constantly together, draw us into separate loneliness with Thyself.

'And when we meet breast to breast, O God, let it be upon Thine own.'

There's always something hidden, something new, something different. Something that you're always fascinated with and anxious to learn more about. A successful marriage is not one in which two people find each other and live happily ever after because they are perfectly matched. A successful marriage is a system by means of which two people who are sinful, two people who are contentious, are so caught by a dream bigger than themselves, that they work throughout the years – in spite of repeated disappointments – they work to make the dream come true.

LOVEWORK ON CHAPTER 9

A picture tells a thousand words

Look at the pictures below for five minutes or so.
Ask yourself, 'Where am I now? Which picture best describes where I am in our relationship?' Note, it is *your* interpretation of the picture that is important.
Each spouse share your answer with your partner.
Ask yourself, 'Where would I like to be? Which picture best describes where I want to be?'
Each spouse share your answer with your partner. Take care to avoid flippancy and you will discover some real depth in this exercise.

Living life to the full

'Live life, then, with a due sense of responsibility, not as men who do not know the meaning and purpose of life but as *those who do*. Make the best use of your time, despite all the difficulties of these days. Don't be vague but firmly grasp what you know to be the will of God. Don't get your stimulus from wine (for there is always the danger of excessive drinking), but let the Spirit stimulate your souls. Express your joy in singing among yourselves psalms and hymns and spiritual songs, making music in your hearts for the ears of God! Thank God at all times for everything, in the name of our Lord Jesus Christ. And "fit in with" each other, because of your common reverence for Christ.'
(EPHESIANS 5:15-21, JBP.)

If only
Erma Bombeck, America's much-loved humorist, said: 'Somebody asked me the other day, if I had my life to live over, would I change anything? No, I answered, but then I began to think . . .

'If I had my life to live over, I would have talked less and listened more.

'If would have invited friends over to dinner even if the carpet was stained and the sofa faded.

'I would have sat on the lawn with my children and not worried about grass stains.

'I would have cried and laughed less while watching television and more while watching life.

'I would have shared more of the responsibility carried by my husband.

'Instead of wishing away nine months of pregnancy, I'd have cherished every moment and realized that the wonderment growing inside me was my only chance in life to assist God in a miracle.

'When my child kissed me impetuously, I would never have said: "Later. Now get washed up for dinner."

'There would have been more I love yous . . . more I'm sorrys . . . but mostly, given one shot at life, I would seize every minute . . . look at it . . . and never give it back.'

When you look back over your life, what would you like to be able to say? Can you say you have lived your life to the full? The apostle Paul thought about it and this was his conclusion: 'The time of my

departure is at hand. I have fought a good fight, I have finished my course, I have kept the faith.' (2 Timothy 4:6, 7, KJV.) Perhaps this summarizes the Christian life in general and Christian marriage in particular: the fight, the finish, and the faith.

The fight
Even before you get married, recognize the reality that marriages are breaking up all around you that had the same glorious beginning as yours. You *can* become a statistic. Marriage is a battleground but the players are not you and your spouse, they are you and temptation. There are things in marriage that you have to fight *off* and things you have to fight *for*. One little boy was asked to recite the ten commandments and when he came to the seventh he said, 'Thou shalt not admit adultery.' Fight off the temptation for lying. Fight off the temptation for adultery.

Then fight for each other's happiness. Fight for each other's reputation. Fight for those evenings together in your marriage. And don't just fight, fight a good fight. Paul said, 'Fight the good fight of faith.' (1 Timothy 6:12, KJV.) Your marriage does not have to end in ruins. Be proactive, be intentional, decide irrevocably that you want victory, and you shall have it.

Fred and Florence's marriage got off to a fairy-tale beginning. They were both hopeless romantics. Wedding fever swept across the high school where Florence was teaching. One of the pupils wrote a letter to *Life* magazine, summing up the excitement of the entire student body. The editors of

Take time out to do things together.

Cinderella wedding
UGLY SISTER'S MARRIAGE

'**Cinderella** got ready to meet Prince Charming at the altar and live happily ever after. It was a perfect night: the wedding of two perfect people in a perfect setting. *But* – after every wedding comes a marriage. Because of our differences in background we had divergent expectations. I thought marriage would be fun, but Fred wanted me to get down to business. When we returned from our honeymoon, Fred put me on a training programme. He wanted me to be the perfect wife, and he worked to teach me how to walk, talk, look, and cook. I thought I knew enough already. I quietly rebelled at his instructions. He persevered and felt that I should be grateful to be so well-trained. The *differences in background* leading to unrealistic expectations drove a wedge into the heart of our marriage. Fred and I were at the bottom. Our marriage was meaningless. Our two sons were hopeless. We had given up on making each other perfect and we had given up on God. Our differences in religion, coupled with our double tragedy, split us apart and left us with no faith at all. Is it possible for two people with different backgrounds and different religions ever to get together? What happens when those with fairy-tale expectations are brought to the harsh realities of hopelessness and death? Is there any force on earth to bind up the wounded and revive those with no love of life?'

FLORENCE LITTAUER, *After Every Wedding Comes a Marriage.*

the magazine were looking for a bride for 'Bride-of-the-Year' and liked what they read. They sent their reporter to Florence and Fred. In the two weeks leading up to the wedding every move was photographed. Florence and Fred couldn't have been happier.

HOW TO CROSS THE FINISH LINE

FINISHERS are people who . . .

Focus on solutions, not problems.

Include their spouse in their plans.

Negotiate, don't dominate.

Include people less fortunate in their plans.

Show patience to each other.

Hold at arm's length outside interference.

Embrace often and keep the romance alive.

Read the Bible, pray alone and together.

Stay faithful – even if they don't feel like it.

The wedding day came and everything went off just right. But their fairy-tale beginning was just that – only a beginning. Some years later Florence Littauer catalogued all that went wrong, and called her book, *After Every Wedding Comes a*

Marriage. Unexpected developments affected the relationship for which even premarital counselling had not prepared them.

Determine early that your marriage is worth fight for. It's not enough to start well – you've got to finish!

The finish
Dr Willard Beecher tells how most people come to marriage believing it is a box full of goodies from which we extract all we need to make us happy. We can take from it as much as we want and it will somehow remain mysteriously full.

Even when the box does empty and the marriage collapses in a heap, we don't learn, we look for another partner who will bring another bottomless box with them so we can empty it.

Marriage is *not* a box full of goodies. The truth of the matter is, marriage is an empty box. There's nothing in it! You see, marriage was never intended to do anything for anybody. People are expected to do something for marriage. Don't try to take out what you did not put in.

There will be disappointments,

Husbands, wives, put something into the box

Put some . . .

smiles into the box
conversation into the box
kind words into the box
admiration into the box
compliments into the box
generosity into the box
flowers into the box
chocolates into the box
romance into the box
love notes into the box
restaurant dinners into the box
hotel reservations into the box.

but *finish the race*. Walt Disney brought out a family film that told of a Jamaican bobsled team who, but for defective equipment, would have won the winter Olympics against tremendous odds. As I saw people accustomed to the sun-kissed Caribbean toiling through the snow, what impressed me most about that historic bobsled team was that they finished the race.

Husband and wife, don't let defective equipment prevent you from finishing the race. Don't allow defects in character, selfishness, or unkind words split up your marriage. Don't let alcohol, adultery, or abuse cause your marriage to be abandoned. Don't let drink, drugs or debauchery cause your marriage to be destroyed. Don't let a television or a computer, a sports programme or a golf course, a newspaper or a pornographic magazine, a colleague or a secre-

The alcoholic and the workaholic are both in danger of destroying their marriages.

tary – don't let *anything* ruin your marriage.

These days you ask a man how Mary is, and he says, 'Mary, who is Mary? It's Jane now, and it's been Susan and Louise in between.' No matter if you married a white Rolls Royce or a red Volkswagen, the same vehicle that you drove into the tunnel is the same vehicle we want to see you in at the end of the tunnel. Put a distance between you and anything that threatens the health of your marriage.

When it dawned on a few of the

Couples often neglect to consider the ground rules of their relationship. They tend to overestimate the extent of mutual understanding and agreement on the rules and goals of their relationship.
The following questionnaire will bring out similarities and differences in your family backgrounds. Where scores are markedly different, discussion may be necessary in order for you to plan your own family system.

FAMILY SYSTEMS TEST

Circle the answer nearest your experience
(O = Often, S = Sometimes, N = Never)

VARIOUS FAMILY RULES, TRADITIONS AND VALUES

	Wife	Husband
As a family we were very health conscious	O S N	O S N
We were early for appointments	O S N	O S N
We made our beds and kept the house tidy	O S N	O S N
We washed the dishes after meals	O S N	O S N
We watched television	O S N	O S N
My parents were open and positive about sexual matters	O S N	O S N
My father had a positive egalitarian attitude towards sexual matters	O S N	O S N
My father was negative and demeaning about the role of women	O S N	O S N
My mother was positive about, and appreciative of men and their role in society	O S N	O S N
Dad willingly helped Mum with the chores	O S N	O S N
We entertained guests and friends in our home	O S N	O S N

STYLES OF AFFECTION

	Wife	Husband
My parents expressed affection to each other	O S N	O S N
My parents showed me love and warmth	O S N	O S N
My parents encouraged feelings of self-worth	O S N	O S N
In crises, family members were supportive	O S N	O S N
My family was very close, sharing together	O S N	O S N
Affection was expressed verbally and physically	O S N	O S N
Compliments/appreciation were generously given	O S N	O S N

COMMUNICATION STYLES

	Wife	Husband
In my family we shared feelings freely	O S N	O S N
In our family there were things we were not permitted to discuss	O S N	O S N
My parents were always ready to listen to each other	O S N	O S N
The mood in our home was one of fun and peace	O S N	O S N

Our home was full of tension	O S N	O S N
We dealt with conflicts immediately and in a positive way	O S N	O S N
My parents encouraged appropriate expression of anger, fear and sadness	O S N	O S N
My parents hid, ridiculed, or discouraged such emotions as anger, fear and sadness	O S N	O S N
In our family we encouraged and affirmed each other	O S N	O S N
We experienced criticism, teasing, and other forms of psychological abuse	O S N	O S N
Both Mum and Dad were fully involved at family counsels	O S N	O S N
Dad did most of the talking at family counsels	O S N	O S N
Mum did most of the talking at family counsels	O S N	O S N
Dad was uncommunicative	O S N	O S N
Mum was uncommunicative	O S N	O S N
We cried freely and were given support	O S N	O S N
We never cried, or it was quickly stopped	O S N	O S N

POWER STYLES

My parents made joint decisions, and our family worked like a team	O S N	O S N
My Father made the decisions	O S N	O S N
My Mother made the decisions	O S N	O S N
Discipline was firm and loving	O S N	O S N
Discipline was harsh	O S N	O S N
Discipline was non-existent	O S N	O S N
My parents encouraged independence and individuality	O S N	O S N
My parents achieved conformity by the use of threats or punishment	O S N	O S N
We children ran the home and did as we pleased	O S N	O S N
My parents accepted and encouraged our individual differences	O S N	O S N
My parents were definitely the leaders	O S N	O S N
Mum and Dad worked as a team	O S N	O S N
Mum and Dad worked against each other	O S N	O S N
Each member of the family was treated equally	O S N	O S N
Mum and Dad had favourites	O S N	O S N
Dad was the head of the home	O S N	O S N
Mum was the head of the home	O S N	O S N
Mum and Dad were fair and open in their decision making	O S N	O S N
Mum and Dad resorted to blackmail against each other to get their own way	O S N	O S N
My mother physically abused us	O S N	O S N
My father physically abused us	O S N	O S N
My father physically abused my mother	O S N	O S N

crowd at that winter Olympics that the Jamaican bobsled team intended to finish the race, you could hear a few handclaps. Pretty soon, as they neared the finish line, those handclaps turned into deafening applause; thousands cheering them on because they had the courage to struggle together to the finish line. As you struggle together towards your finish line, there are some people cheering you on. You won't always see them, but they are individuals who have themselves struggled and been victorious. They want you to finish the race. Hebrews 12:1, 2 (LB) says it this way:

'Since we have such a huge crowd of men of faith watching us from the grandstands, let us strip off anything that slows us down or holds us back, and especially those sins that wrap themselves so tightly around our feet and trip us up; and let us run with patience the particular race that God has set before us. Keep your eyes on Jesus, our leader and instructor . . . . If you want to keep from becoming fainthearted and weary, think about his patience as sinful men did such terrible things to him.'

Don't just begin well; stay together and finish the race. 'And I am sure that God who began the good work within you will keep right on helping you grow in his

grace until his task within you is finally finished on that day when Jesus Christ returns.' (Philippians 1:6, LB.)

The faith
Whether your marriage is going through smooth or rough waters, the only thing that can guarantee lasting commitment is faith in God.

Everything was set. All the runners were lined up. The starter had his stopwatch and gun. I surveyed my junior school opposition. Three good runners. They were going to have to be more than just good to beat me. He'll come fourth . . . . 'On your marks . . . .' He'll come third . . . . 'Get set . . . .' He'll come second . . . . 'Go!' As I took my first step forward, I slipped and fell flat on my face. I got up. I saw the other runners way ahead of me. I was furious. Try as I might, I only managed to overtake one person. I ran in next to last. Ran like a madman. But, oh, how I wanted the race to start all over again.

You see, when you've slipped in the race, what you need is a new start. With Jesus by our side, we *can* start again! The Bible says, 'For if a man is in Christ he becomes a new person altogether – the past is finished and gone, everything has become fresh and new' (2 Corinthians 5:17, JBP).

Adept

That good news of a new beginning is worth passing on. It's too good to keep to myself. It's not enough that just my family is happy; I belong to a larger family. The African extended family is marvellous to behold, but I belong to a family that's even broader and more adept, not because of anybody in it, but because it's Christ's body. It's

'If a man is in Christ he becomes a new person altogether. . . .'

When both partners share a forever friendship with God the marriage is built on the best foundation of all.

called the family of God. All our brothers and sisters in the Church form the new family with Christ as our elder Brother. We are a family in church before we are a family at home. This is a new, more excellent way.

Tertullian was a famous non-biblical writer of the second century. He saw something special in the marriage of two people who also claimed to be married to a man called Jesus Christ, and this is what he wrote:

'How beautiful is the marriage of two Christians; two who are one in hope, one in desire, one in the way of life they follow, one in the religion they practise . . . . Nothing divides them, either in flesh or spirit. They pray together, they worship together, they fast together; instructing one another, encouraging one another, strengthening one another. Side by side they visit God's church and partake of God's banquet; side by side they face difficulties and persecution, share their consolations. They have no secrets from one another; they never shun each other's company; they never bring sorrow to each other's hearts.'

Tertullian was right, but he didn't tell the whole story.

Christian marriage means more than just populating the globe with happy families. We have been adopted into the family of God (Romans 11). In the same way, Christian families are called to go into the highways and byways and

adopt others into their families. Those others will comprise, in particular, the oppressed and the despised, the least, the last, and the lost. Adoption agencies are crying out for black parents in particular to adopt or foster black children. You may literally adopt or foster or you may sponsor a child, through a Christian agency, for example.

Adopt

One church in Ypsilanti, Michigan, a university town, has an adopt-a-student programme, so that Christian students have a home away from home. Another church has an adopt-a-grandparent programme. Still another church announced that they were having a father-son retreat. There was general rejoicing until it was noticed that one small boy was head bowed with tears in his eyes. When they inquired, they discovered he had no father. A godly single man said, 'I'll be your father for the camp.'

When we call a feast, they are the people whom we are to invite first (Luke 14:12-14.) The elderly, students, single adults, single mothers, bachelor fathers, the disabled, the unpopular. The Christian family life message says, 'Whosoever will, let them come.'

With this new community having all things in common, the Lord will add daily to the family of God. Women's status will be affirmed in the family of God. Men will see Christ as their model for singleness, marriage and fathering. The hearts of the fathers will turn to their children. Children will feel included in family and church

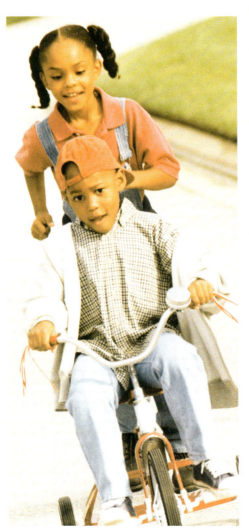

because Jesus said, 'Allow the little children to come to me.' Divisions in the church because of age, sex and race will disappear. Suspicion, prejudice, and racism will be eliminated, for we are now controlled by the Gospel. There will be one Lord, one faith, one baptism. Wealth will be shared, poverty reduced. The family of God will be one, even as Christ and the Father are one.

The world will recognize that God has sent Christ into the world, for such a demonstration of unity will shake and shock the earth. The world will know we are Christians by our love, the Gospel commission will be fulfilled, and Jesus will come. We will then realize anew that the purpose of our singleness or married state was never our pleasure but always His purpose. We will cast our crowns at His feet, saying, 'Thou art worthy, O Lord, to receive glory and honour and power: for thou hast created all things, and for thy pleasure they are and were created.' Revelation 4:11, KJV.

Adapt

Reader, your marriage may be struggling because your spouse has not turned out as you expected. Adapt. Perhaps you are having difficulty trusting your spouse. You may be wondering if indeed you made a mistake in your choice of marriage partner. Just adapt. Others have a happy marriage and can't imagine having any of the problems that some of your friends have. Don't become complacent.

We want you to know the Bible is rich in resources for a married couple to draw on. The Bible is full of weak people who discovered that they could be strong, and strong people who discovered that they could be weak. If you are a Christian, do not act as if the Bible had never been written. It was written for us, yes *us*, with our helpless and sometimes hopeless situations in mind. It is our prayer that your spouse will, with you, lay hold of God's promises, such as the one below. And we believe that one day you will hear God say, 'Somebody's life was enriched because of you two. Well done, thou good and faithful servants. Enter thou into the joys of thy Lord.' Let's keep the faith.

'All these things happened to them as examples – as object lessons to us – to warn us against doing the same things; they were written down so that we could read about them and learn from them in these last days as the world nears its end. So be careful.

'If you are thinking, "Oh, I would never behave like that" – let this be a warning to you. For you too may fall into sin. But remember this – the wrong desires that come into your life aren't anything new and different. Many others have faced exactly the same problems before you.

'And no temptation is irresistible. You can trust God to keep the temptation from becoming so strong that you can't stand up against it, for he has promised this and will do what he says. He will show you how to escape temptation's power so that you can bear up patiently against it.'

1 CORINTHIANS 10:11-13, LB.

LOVEWORK ON CHAPTER 10

Our marriage goals

What would you like to do to strengthen your marriage?
Make a list together, such as

To consider who we can adopt into the family that God has blessed us with.
To be more regular and creative in our family worship.
To be more knowledgeable and creative in our sexual relationship.
To have regular times away from home together.
To have specific functions in the ministry of our church.
To become more united and responsible in our finances.
To be involved in local community or charity work.

Below are a few passages that we believe will strengthen you as you pursue your goal of having a

TOTAL MARRIAGE

May God bless you.

SITUATION	PROMISE
When you are worried and anxious	1 PETER 5:7; PHILIPPIANS 4:6, 7; MATTHEW 6:25, 34.
When you need forgiveness and understanding	COLOSSIANS 3:12-14; LUKE 6:37; MATTHEW 6:14, 15.
When you need guidance in decision-making	PSALM 16:11; ISAIAH 58:11; PROVERBS 3:5, 6; PSALM 73:24.
When you are in difficulty or trouble	PSALM 46:1; ROMANS 8:28; JOHN 14:27; PSALM 27:14.
When you are angry and upset	EPHESIANS 4:26, 31; ECCLESIASTES 7:9; PSALM 37:8.
When communication gets bitter	EPHESIANS 4:29; COLOSSIANS 4:6; PROVERBS 15:1.
When temptation is strong	1 CORINTHIANS 10:13; JAMES 1:12; MATTHEW 26:41.
When you are afraid	PSALM 34:4; PSALM 27:1; JOSHUA 1:9; 2 TIMOTHY 1:7.
When children try your patience	PROVERBS 22:6; EPHESIANS 6:4; COLOSSIANS 3:21.
When you feel like giving up	PSALM 42:11; 2 CORINTHIANS 12:9; COLOSSIANS 1:11.

INDEX

ABORTION, 104, 106
Abuse, 106, 107
Abusive fathers, 112
Active listening, 74-77
Adam and Eve, 15-18, 20, 25
Adolescents, discipline of, 102-104
 their future, 111
Adoption, 106, 170
African family, 13
AIDS, 92-98
Appreciate your wife, 145
Arguments, 69-85
Autobiography, poem, 132

BABY, premature, 121-123
Battered husbands, home for, 21
Bible, the, 11
 and singleness, 41- 43
Biblical model, 13
Born again, 18

CHRISTIAN faith, the, 18
Christian love, 10, 11
Christian marriage, 58
 foundation for, 17
Child abuse, parents' responsibility, 112-114
Children, Home Rules for, 123
 gift of marriage, 100-126
 in second marriages, 131
 on loan, 116-118
Child's Ten Commandments, 105
Church, the, 8
Climax, in sex, 89, 90
Clitoris, 88
Cohabitation, 38, 39

Commitment, 10, 11, 29, 72
 in conflict, 70
 to Jesus Christ, 17, 18
Communication, compatibility and commitment, 144-152
 barriers to, 148, 149
 in marriage, 72
Condoms, 95
Conflict management, 69-85
Contraception, 104, 106
Contract, 17, 18
Counsel to parents, 102-104
Couples, perfect, 9
Courting, 9
Covenant marriage, 17, 18, 40
Creation, 15, 20, 21
Criticism, 70
Cultural variations in marriage, 12-14

DATING, healthy attitude to, 48
Depression, because single, 35, 36
Devotional life, for the single, 48
Dialogue techniques, 84-85
Discipline, preventative/ redemptive, 102
Divided home, 34
Divine triangle, 37, 38
Divorce, in Scripture, 129
 rates, African/West Indian, 128, 129
 recovering from, 131, 132
Dominion, unholy, 15
Dowry, 60

EJACULATION, 90
 premature, 91
 retarded, 91
Erection, of penis, 88
Erogenous zones, 88, 89
Equality, 16
Excitement, in sex, 89
Exclusive commitment, 147-149
Expectations of the single, 46-49
Extended family, 13

FAMILY, African, 13-15
 American, 13
 God's purpose for, 17, 18
 Systems, 58-60

Test, 164, 165
 Western, 12
First baby, authors', 119-123
First man/woman, 20
Finishers, 160
Five levels of communication, 72
Forgiveness, 11
Former relationships, unmourned, 130
Foreplay, 86-88
Functions of marriage, 13

GOALS, for the single, 48
God, 11
 the Helper, 15
 of the single, 41-43
God's plan, for your life, 46
 in marriage, 37, 38
Grief, in African society, 136-138
Group marriage, 58, 59

HANDICAPPED child, the, 118, 119
Headship, 50-56
Heaven's Special Child, poem, 118
Helper, 15, 22
HIV, 92-98
Home rules for children, 123
Husband, ideal, 8
 as manager, 15

IDEAL marriage, 8, 9
Image of God, 22
Immune system, 93
Impotence, 90, 91
Incompatibility, 144
In-laws, 60-66
Intercourse, pain on, 91, 92
Intimacy, 37-40
'I will be with you', quote, 151

JESUS Christ, model of love, 12
Joy of sex, 88, 89

KEEPING the flame alive, 140
Kin groups, 13

LABOLA (bride price), 60

Leadership, and men, 52-54
Listening, 74-77
Loneliness, in singleness, 43-46
Love, and forgiveness, 10, 12
  at first sight, 25
  commitment, 39, 40
  ideal in Bible, 8
  keys to, 25, 26-30
  mystery of, 22, 24
  spontaneous, 18
  what is it? 23

MAJORITY cultures, 13
Male supremacy, 15
Man's tears, a, 54
Marital relationship, basis for, 25
Marital sex, God's gift, 86
Marriage, American view of, 13
  biblical concept of, 15, 16
  enrichment, programme,
    134, 135
  factors, 13
  of Christ, 8
  relationships, 8, 22, 24
Mate selection, 58, 59
Meaningful dialogue, for parents,
  114-119
Minority, 12, 13
Monogamy, 13, 58-60
Mr/Mrs Right, 21, 22
Mutuality, 15
Mutual submission, 52-58

NEW AFRICAN, article, 127, 128
New deal, in marriage, 8
New family, in Christ, 168
Nuclear family, 13

ONE and only, the, 47, 48
Orgasm, 90-92
Other men/women, 11

PARENTAL expectations of
  children, 117
Parents' responsibility to
  children, 102, 104
Permanent relationship, 9
Perversions of creation, 15
Polyandry/polygamy, 58
Polygamy, in Africa/America, 59
Prayer, in marriage, 25, 29

Premarital counselling, 9, 24
  relationship weekends, 133
  sex, 24
Prescription for dull marriage,
  153
Promiscuity, 13
Promise, ours/God's, 12
Psalmist David, 11
Put God first, 154

RAPE, 108, 109
Recovery from Divorce, 131
Redemption, 16, 17
Remarriage, after death of
  spouse, 137
Respect, 24
Responsibility for chores, 68
Results of sin, 15, 16

SACRED circle, 147
Safe sex, 95
Scripture and your rights, 11
Second/subsequent marriages,
  129-132
Serial monogamy, 60
Service, happiness from, 11
Self-esteem, 34-36
Seven deadly steps to infidelity,
  139
Seven Important Things to Say,
  147
Sex, education, 37, 38
  God's plan for, 45
  marital, 86, 87
Sexual dysfunctions, 90-92
  immorality, 20, 118, 119
  intercourse, 86-90
  fulfilment, God's plan, 48, 49
  response, stages of, 88-90
Sexually-abused child, the,
  112, 113
Sickness and health, in, 22
Single, all right to be, 49
  people, categories, 32-34
  social life of, 48
Singleness, 32-49
  benefits of, 41-43
  in Bible, 48
Solitude, 45
Solving conflicts, 79-83
Stages in sexual arousal, 88-90

Strengths, in marriage, 19
Stress and illness, Life Crises,
  142-143
Strong family, 70-72
Submission, in marriage,
  56, 58

TEENAGE years, 108-110
Teens, Five Messages for, 111
Temptation, 172
Ten Ways to Say I Love You,
  145
Togetherness, 70, 72
Trial marriage, 39, 40
Types, of personality, 19

UNBELIEVING partner, 127
Unique gift of God, 113
Unity, after marriage, 35
Unsupervised hours, children,
  102-104

VAGINAL tightening, 91
Vasocongestion, 88, 89

WEDDING night, 10
Western family, 12, 13
Widowhood, 135-137
Wife, abuse of, 21
  as assistant manager, 15
  in Bible, 8
Woman, man's property?
  22, 24
Worldly love, 10, 11

YOU be the counsellor, 62
Your communication style
  (test), 152

PHOTOGRAPHERS' COPYRIGHTS

ADOBE IMAGE LIBRARY
1, 5, 6, 7, 14, 26, 28, 33, 35, 36, 38, 42, 44, 47, 49, 51, 53, 55, 57, 59, 65, 73, 77, 78, 79, 82, 87, 88, 89, 90, 98, 101, 103, 104, 105, 113, 115, 116, 119, 123, 125, 126, 128, 130, 131, 134, 138, 141, 143, 145, 146, 150, 154, 157, 158, 160–161, 162, 163, 166, 167, 170, 171.

AUTUMN HOUSE
5(top), 6, 7(top), 9, 10, 16, 21, 24, 26, 27, 30, 34, 39, 43, 54, 61, 63, 67, 70, 74, 84, 85, 106, 115, 124, 127, 134, 135, 149, 163(bottom), 169.

COREL IMAGES
12.

JEFFREY BROWN
121, 122.

LUDWIG WERNER BINEMANN
69, 109, 114, 136, 137, 153, 168.

SCIENCE PHOTO LIBRARY
93, 94.

SUSANNA BURTON
110.